baby
sign language
basics

Also by Monta Z. Briant

Baby Sign Language Basics:
Early Communication for Hearing Babies and Toddlers Instructional DVD

Baby Sign Language Basics Flash Cards:
A Deck of 50 American Sign Language (ASL) Cards

Sign, Sing, and Play!
Fun Signing Activities for You and Your Baby (book)

The Sign, Sing, and Play Kit

"Songs for Little Hands" Activity Guide & CD (with Susan Z)

All of the above are available at your local bookstore,
or maybe ordered by visiting:
Hay House USA: **www.hayhouse.com**®
Hay House Australia: **www.hayhouse.com.au**
Hay House UK: **www.hayhouse.co.uk**
Hay House South Africa: **www.hayhouse.co.za**
Hay House India: **www.hayhouse.co.in**

baby
sign language
basics

Early Communication for
Hearing Babies and Toddlers

New & Expanded Edition

Monta Z. Briant

HAY HOUSE, INC.
Carlsbad, California • New York City
London • Sydney • Johannesburg
Vancouver • Hong Kong • New Delhi

Published and distributed in the United States by: Hay House, Inc.: www.hayhouse.com • *Published and distributed in Australia by:* Hay House Australia Pty. Ltd.: www.hayhouse.com.au • *Published and distributed in the United Kingdom by:* Hay House UK, Ltd.: www.hayhouse.co.uk • *Published and distributed in the Republic of South Africa by:* Hay House SA (Pty), Ltd.: www.hayhouse.co.za • *Distributed in Canada by:* Raincoast: www.raincoast.com • *Published in India by:* Hay House Publishers India: www.hayhouse.co.in

Editorial supervision: Jill Kramer • *Design:* Amy Gingery • *Interior photos of Monta:* Greg Bertolini • *Photos of children:* Paul Briant, Susan Zelinsky, Mike Jobe, Mike Zelinsky, and Jennifer Vignale • *I Love You Hand and Foot Photos:* Bill Pitcher • *Illustrations:* Diana Hocking, **www.dianahocking.com** and Summer McStravick

Library of Congress Cataloging-in-Publication Data

Briant, Monta Z.
  Baby sign language basics : early communication for hearing babies and toddlers / Monta Z. Briant. -- New & expanded ed.
      p. cm.
    ISBN-13: 978-1-4019-2159-0. 1. Nonverbal communication in children. 2. Interpersonal communication in children. 3. Infants--Language. 4. Child rearing. 5. American Sign Language. I. Title.
    BF723.C57B75 2008
    419'.1--dc22   2008004507

ISBN: 978-1-4019-2159-0

16 15 14 13   10 9 8 7
1st edition (revised version), June 2009
7th edition, July 2013

Printed in the United States of America

For my own signing babies, Sirena and Aiden;
and for my loving husband, Paul. I certainly could
not have done any of this without you!

✖ ✖ ✖

contents

Preface ix

Introduction xi

PART I: ABOUT BABY SIGN LANGUAGE

Chapter 1:   Baby Sign Language Saves the Day,
Keeping Elephants at Bay 3

Chapter 2:   What Is Baby Sign Language?...5

Chapter 3:   The Benefits...9

Chapter 4:   Frequently Asked Questions 15

PART II: GETTING STARTED

Chapter 5:   When Can You Start?...31

Chapter 6:   How to Sign to Your Baby..35

Chapter 7:   Choosing First Signs 41

PART III: NOW YOU'RE SIGNING!

Chapter 8: Lifesaver Signs 49

Chapter 9: Attention-Getting Strategies 55

Chapter 10: Positive Reinforcement 63

Chapter 11: Signing Mistakes 65

Chapter 12: Made-Up Signs 71

Chapter 13: Setting Limits 75

Chapter 14: Combining Signs 79

Chapter 15: Stumbling Blocks 81

Chapter 16: Including Caregivers, Family, and Friends 87

Chapter 17: Is There Signing After Talking? 95

Chapter 18: The Greatest Gift 99

PART IV: SIGNING FOR FUN

Chapter 19: Signing and Playing 105

Chapter 20: Storytime 111

Chapter 21: Sing, Sign, and Rhyme! 115

APPENDIX

Signing Vocabulary..127

    • *The Manual Alphabet* 131

    • *ASL Numbers*...132

Acknowledgments...453

Resources 455

Endnotes 463

About the Author...465

preface

When I was pregnant with my daughter, Sirena, my mother attended a baby sign language class through her local community college. I thought it was pretty funny that my mom was taking a parenting class 34 years after she had me, but I was also intrigued by the idea of being able to communicate with my baby before she could talk—what would she say? There was no such class in my community at the time, so I was excited to hear what my mom had learned when she next came to visit me in San Diego.

Little could I have known that signing with Sirena would be the most amazing experience for my husband and me, to the point that we don't know what we would have done without it! Of course, signing with our baby reduced frustration by taking a lot of the guesswork out of parenting and helped us meet Sirena's needs more easily, but there was so much more. The best part was getting to know our baby on a level that wouldn't have been possible otherwise. And once Sirena began signing back, I became a "baby sign language evangelist," chasing down everyone I saw with a baby to tell them about signing with babies: in the supermarket checkout line, on walks, and at the playground. I wanted to share this incredible gift with every new parent.

I've since found a more efficient means of spreading the good news than accosting anyone pushing a stroller. In order to stay at home with Sirena, I decided to teach baby sign language classes. My company, Baby Sign Language Workshops, offers parent/teacher focused workshops and parent/child signing classes throughout San Diego County.

This book will start you and your baby on an amazing journey of communication and discovery—a discovery of each other *and* a discovery of your new world together.

Your baby is trying to tell you something . . . so don't wait to communicate!

introduction

As a new or prospective parent, you may be thinking that signing with your baby sounds pretty neat, but you're also probably thinking that you'll be incredibly busy with a new baby, so learning sign language won't be at the top of your list of priorities when the dirty diapers and strained peas start to fly.

Let me assure you that signing with your baby is easy—it's certainly much easier than *not* signing with your baby! Although we call it "baby sign language," and the signs we recommend using are actual American Sign Language (ASL) signs, you don't need to become fluent in ASL in order to communicate with your little one. Think of the book you now hold in your hands as the "baby talk" version of signing, and if a six-month-old can learn to do this, so can you.

Baby Sign Language Basics includes everything you need to get started right now. Along with more than 300 of the most useful signs (which are located in the Appendix), you'll find developmental information, strategies for getting your baby's attention, and engaging playtime signing activities and songs. There's even a Resources section in the back to help you look up more signs when you need them! When using this book, watch for words highlighted in **BOLD CAPS,** as they represent the signed vocabulary words you'll find in the Appendix.

The original version of *Baby Sign Language Basics,* published in 2004, was a small book designed to be carried in the diaper bag; and as of this writing, hundreds of thousands of parents have used it to begin communicating with their preverbal children.

While the small size has no doubt been one of the secrets of *Basics'* success, many moms and dads have told me that they'd like to have a book with more signs. So for all those brilliant parents and babies who just can't get enough, I give you *Baby Sign Language Basics*—the *new and expanded* edition!

✻ ✻ ✻

[**Author's Note:** In order to avoid the awkward he/she construction, I've opted to alternate the use of the masculine and feminine pronouns throughout this book. Please note that the same information applies universally to both girls and boys.]

part I

about baby sign language

chapter 1

Baby Sign Language Saves the Day, Keeping Elephants at Bay

My then ten-month-old daughter, Sirena, had always been easy to put to bed, so when she clung to me and cried one warm night, I wondered what could be wrong. Was she suddenly old enough to protest going to sleep?

I looked at her and asked, "What's wrong?" simultaneously shrugging my shoulders and lifting my hands, palms up, in the natural gesture that is also the American Sign Language (ASL) sign for **WHAT?**

My tiny daughter immediately pointed to the open window and waved one hand in an arc out from her face, a gesture that I recognized as her approximation of the ASL sign for **ELEPHANT.** Now, I already knew that Sirena was terrified of elephants, expressing this when she saw them at the zoo and on video—even a cute, fluffy hand puppet wasn't okay.

I'd also noticed that recently Sirena had begun signing **ELEPHANT** whenever she heard a car alarm or siren, which she'd apparently decided were noises made by elephants, so I followed her gaze to the window that, until this evening, had been closed while she slept. Suddenly, I saw my urban neighborhood through my baby's eyes: a noisy place full of trumpeting elephants who were out of sight yet clearly around each corner, just waiting to reach or climb through a window carelessly left open!

I closed and locked the window and shut the blinds, and my sweet little girl went happily to sleep.

For the first time, it really hit me just how valuable baby sign language was. If Sirena hadn't been able to communicate her specific fear through signing, I might have, in my ignorance, left her alone, crying in her crib, terrified of the car-alarm "elephants" outside.

✳ ✳ ✳   ✳ ✳ ✳

chapter 2

What Is Baby Sign Language?

Baby sign language is the practice of using symbolic gestures to enhance your verbal interactions with your baby. Using symbolic gestures is something all human beings do naturally—for example, when your baby raises her arms to be picked up or when she points at something to draw your attention to it.

Not only is it completely natural to use symbolic gestures, it's nearly impossible to stop yourself from doing so—I mean, imagine trying to give directions to people without using your hands! You'd probably have to sit on them to keep from gesturing, and you'd very likely find your head or entire body jerking or leaning in the direction of what you're describing (for example, "Turn left at the Shell station, and turn right at the 7-Eleven"). By the same token, if you use particular gestures to enhance certain words when you interact with your baby, she'll learn to use the same gestures you do, so communication will come along a lot better.

In this book, we'll use ASL signs as our symbolic gestures. While it *is* possible to use made-up signs, I feel that ASL signs are preferable for a number of reasons. First of all, if you're going to take the time to teach your baby something, why not teach her a skill she can use for a lifetime, rather than something that will just be discarded as soon as she learns to talk? At age two, Sirena was already able to use her signs to communicate with a deaf mother and her hearing/signing child, as well as with an adult who has Down syndrome and uses some signing.

Another good reason to stick with ASL is all the wonderful teaching resources that are available. Once your baby begins signing in earnest, she'll start asking you for signs for everything; and even though this new, expanded edition has more than 300 signs, no one book can include every sign your baby might want to learn. At your local library, you can pick up an ASL dictionary containing thousands of signs, along with ASL children's books that not only allow your child to see the sign on the page, but also serve as a parent's "cheat sheet" as you read and sign the story to your son or daughter. There are also wonderful, free resources available online where you can find a wealth of signs. Be sure to check the Resources section in the back of this book for these!

Last, but certainly not least, ASL is being used with increasing frequency in child-care and preschool programs, and even into the elementary and high-school years. Signing in infant and toddler programs cuts down on aggressive behavior, including hitting and biting; it works wonderfully as a "language bridge" among children who speak different languages; and it helps to include special-needs children with their peers. Imagine seeing your child sign with a deaf or hard-of-hearing friend! And signing (finger spelling) while practicing vocabulary words has been shown to increase spelling test scores by 60 percent in elementary schoolchildren. There are so many benefits on so many levels here. Speaking of which, the next chapter explains these benefits in detail.

chapter 3

The Benefits

During their comprehensive research that was funded by the National Institutes of Health, Drs. Linda Acredolo and Susan Goodwyn found that signing with hearing babies had many short- *and* long-term advantages. More than 140 families participating in their study were randomly assigned to either a signing or non-signing (control) group. The groups were equal with respect to family education/income level and the children's gender, birth order, and tendency to vocalize or verbalize words. Acredolo and Goodwyn found that the signing group enjoyed the following benefits:

1. Signing empowers babies to communicate very early in life. Signing enables babies to communicate *specific* things, such as fears or location of pain. Even more amazing, signing allows babies to bring up topics of conversation that interest them—something that no amount of crying can do!

2. Signing increases self-esteem. Signing allows babies to begin participating as contributing members of the household early on. You'll be absolutely thrilled when your baby shares his thoughts with you, and your *baby* will be thrilled that you understand and value what he has to say. Signing gives your child an early measure of self-sufficiency by allowing him a way to communicate his needs, feelings, and observations.

3. Signing reduces frustration for parents and babies alike. Babies who sign experience less frustration and crying, and fewer tantrums. It isn't hard to see why. Imagine not being able to communicate even your most basic needs to the only person who could provide for them—you'd cry, too!

4. Signing builds language skills. Signing babies tend to talk earlier and build vocabulary faster than their nonsigning peers. On average, children who signed as babies have 50 more spoken words in their vocabularies by age two than children who didn't sign. (That's not even counting all the *signed* words they're using by then!) The study also found that by the age of 36 months, the signing children were speaking at the 47-month age level—nearly a year ahead of their nonsigning peers![1]

5. Signing increases bonding and enriches parent/child interactions. You'll naturally have a richer and closer relationship with your baby when you have two-way communication. Signing also enables you to be a more compassionate caregiver—since you can understand your baby's specific fears and concerns, this will help build a foundation of trust between you and your child.

6. Signing creates a window into your child's mind and personality. For moms and dads, this is the best benefit, as far as I'm concerned—it's the parents' reward for signing with their baby. I can't adequately describe the wonder you'll feel as your baby begins to share his fresh interpretation of the world with you. Your little one misses nothing, and he'll show you things that you've walked past a thousand times without noticing. We adults are so rushed most of the time that we run through this beautiful world with tunnel vision. Signing with your baby will force you to slow down once in a while and see through his eyes; you'll find that it's a bright, new, and wonderful place full of amazing things to look at and explore. Only by signing with your baby will you get such an early glimpse into your child's universe.

7. Signing allows you to see just how smart your baby really is. Oftentimes, parents underestimate how much their very young child is capable of understanding. By the time Sirena was 15 months old, I was talking to her about pretty much anything that I didn't think would scare her, and her questions and level of reasoning amazed me on a daily basis.

One week, Sirena and I made two visits to the home of a pregnant neighbor. I tried to explain to my then 15-month-old daughter about the baby in our neighbor's tummy and that when it came out, our neighbor would be a mommy. Sirena looked worried, and I hoped I hadn't traumatized her somehow. I wondered what she was thinking.

A few days later, after the baby had arrived, Sirena and I walked down the block again to see the new mother and baby and to deliver a casserole. My daughter acted shy and wore a worried little furrow in her brow. On the way home, as I tried to explain about the birth again, Sirena stopped me. "Mama," she said, and then signed **BABY BIRD** and the sign she used for **OUT** (as in "take out").

I could scarcely believe my eyes. My 15-month-old was asking me if a baby coming out of a mommy's tummy was anything like a baby bird coming out of an egg. "Yes, you're right, honey!" I assured her. "They're both being born. A chick is born out of an egg, and babies are born out of their mommy's tummy."

The furrow in Sirena's brow instantly disappeared. She hadn't been worried at all—she'd just been thinking very hard. It's amazing that she didn't have smoke coming out of her ears!

Imagine if Sirena had been forced to wait until she could actually *say* the words necessary to ask this question. How frustrating! And how unfortunate to miss such a perfect learning opportunity. Children learn most effectively when lessons are tied in with things that are already of interest to them, so signing allows them to ask questions about their interests and observations long before they can talk.

8. Signing Increases IQ. As a follow-up to their study, Acredolo and Goodwyn tested the original participants' IQ when the children turned eight years old. Their findings showed that the kids who had signed as babies scored an average of 12 points higher than the children in the control groups, with the signers having a mean IQ of 114 (75th percentile) versus the nonsigners' mean score of 102 (53rd percentile).[2]

In addition, signing raises literacy in school-age children.[3] Signing has been proven to boost early literacy skills for success in reading, writing, vocabulary, spelling, and memory by adding visual and kinesthetic emphasis to auditory input. In other words, kids learn more effectively when they combine hearing *and* "doing" words with their hands! Everyone comprehends things better when given the opportunity to actually do a task rather than just reading or hearing about it.

Still not convinced? Hopefully, the next chapter will help dispel any remaining reservations you have.

Chapter 4

Frequently Asked Questions

Q. What if I already know what my baby wants?

A. Babies *are* born with an effective means of communicating their basic needs—*they cry*. When your baby cries, you go through a process of elimination: Is she hungry, wet, tired, or in pain? Usually, after a few tries, you'll hit the right one and she'll stop crying. This, coupled with a good helping of "parent's intuition," actually enables you to meet your baby's basic needs pretty well. So why should you sign?

First of all, signing with your baby saves you a lot of time and lost sleep. Let's say she's crying in the middle of the night. You go to your little angel and nurse and change her. The crying stops while you nurse, but then it starts right up again. After about 45 minutes of this, you get concerned. Is your baby in pain? Is it an ear infection? An intestinal blockage? A burst appendix? Good heavens! Should you take her to the emergency room?

Signing empowers your baby to communicate *specific* things, such as "I have pain in my left ear," "My tummy hurts," or "There's an elephant in my closet!" If your child can indicate to you that she has pain in her left ear, then you could call your pediatrician, who may be able to give you some home-care advice that will ease her discomfort and get you both through until the morning. But imagine rushing your baby to the ER in the middle of the night when all you really needed to do was show her that there was no elephant in her closet!

Q. What's the point—won't my baby talk soon anyway?

A. Well, this depends on what you mean by "soon." Soon can seem like a long time when your child is trying to communicate with you by screaming, throwing things, and banging his head against the wall. In general, most babies don't even use "Mama" and "Dada" to the right parent until they're at least 11 months old, and a 12-month-old who uses two more words *in addition to* "Mama" and "Dada" is considered in the advanced minority.

There's a lot of variation between individual children when it comes to speech development, but the average age for first speech is considered to occur at about 12 months, give or take a couple months. Having said that, there's no way to know in advance at what age *your* baby will begin speaking. In fact, there are many kids who have no words until 2 or even 3 years of age, especially boys.

Even after your child does begin talking, it takes quite some time to go from first words to intelligible conversation; and signing not only helps your baby communicate what he can't say, but it also helps him clarify the meaning of what he *is* saying once he starts verbalizing. A child who says "Da" to mean "dog," "Daddy," and "done" can make his meaning clearer by signing while he speaks. Children are encouraged to verbalize *more* when they see that their intended meaning is understood. Eventually, as the child's verbalization of "dog," "Daddy," and "done" become clearer, he'll drop those signs and simply say the words.

Q. Do I have to learn a whole new language?

A. Not at all. As I mentioned earlier, we call this "baby sign language" because it's the "baby talk" version of signing. Think about going on a grand European vacation: Would you learn the language of every country you intended to visit? Of course not! But you'd probably try to brush up on a few useful words and phrases for each country you planned to travel to, right? You wouldn't sound very eloquent to the native speakers of those languages, but at least you'd be able to get your basic needs met.

When starting to sign with your baby, I suggest choosing between six and ten words to start with and adding more as you feel you're both ready. Parents of young children are *extremely* busy people; and this is exactly why you need early, effective, two-way communication. By empowering your child to communicate her needs, you can ward off frustration and temper tantrums, creating calm and peace in your household, and actually have *more* quality time left to spend with your baby.

Q. How do I respond to other family members who tell me that I shouldn't sign with my baby?

A. Well-meaning family members might be concerned that signing with the baby may be harmful. This belief could be from your spouse or from one of the baby's grandparents, for example. The best way to combat this is by informing them and including them. If you can, ask them to read this book, and show them a few simple signs to use with your child. Better yet, persuade them to come to a signing class with you and your child so you can all learn together! Tell them how important they are in your baby's life and that it would be fun to spend this special time together. Going to a class is especially good because it allows the other person to see that this isn't just some harebrained scheme of yours, and that there are plenty of other perfectly normal parents and babies learning to sign together these days.

Q. How will I find the time to teach my baby?

A. "Teaching" your baby to sign can be compared to teaching your baby to talk. You don't need to put special time aside for signing lessons any more than you would for speaking lessons. As a matter of fact, it's absolutely essential that your baby doesn't suspect that you're trying to teach something "special" or "extra." Signing should be incorporated naturally into your normal day-to-day routines and playtime.

Q. Will signing inhibit my baby's language development?

A. Signing won't inhibit your baby's language development any more than crawling will inhibit his learning to walk. In fact, research shows that babies who sign generally talk sooner and build vocabulary more quickly than their nonsigning peers. In their long-term study, Drs. Linda Acredolo and Susan Goodwyn found that by age 36 months, children who signed as babies were talking at the 47-month age level, putting them nearly a year ahead of their nonsigning peers.[1] Once your baby is physically developed enough to walk, he'll no longer crawl, as walking is a much more efficient means of getting from point A to point B. The same is true of signing and talking—once your baby can say a word clearly enough to make his meaning understood, he'll stop using the sign for that word. When a child's vocal apparatus is sufficiently developed, plain talking is a lot easier (and you can even do it with your hands full!).

Even when your baby is very young, signing enhances his language development by increasing word recognition. Imagine looking at your six-month-old and asking him, "Do you want to eat?" Now imagine doing the same thing, but this time you *sign* the word **EAT** at the same time you *say* "eat." The sign for **EAT** is made by going through the motion of putting something small into your mouth. Even at nine months of age, children generally recognize only about five to six spoken words, so can you see what a powerful hint your baby is getting when you sign *and* speak at the same time?

Q. But a friend of mine told me that one of her co-workers signed with her baby, and now the two-year-old boy signs but won't talk! My friend says it must be the signing that's causing the baby's delayed speech—why should he talk if he can just use his hands? She thinks that I'm crazy to consider signing with my child!

A. Ah, it's the mysterious "friend of a friend"—the stuff of urban legends!

Within the population as a whole, about 10 percent of children will have a speech delay for one reason or another. Many times there's never a specific reason found for the delay; and one day, lo and behold, the child just starts talking.

So, it's quite possible that a baby who signed could later be diagnosed with a speech delay. This would simply be due to the fact that out of every ten people, one will be affected by this whether or not he signed.

Let's say that your pediatrician diagnoses a speech delay in your child and refers you to a speech-language pathologist (SLP) for treatment. Most specialists in this field will employ *signing* with your son or daughter as a method of treatment in order to *encourage* speech development and reduce frustration. Obviously, these physicians wouldn't prescribe signing if it would further delay speech, right? Signing does just the opposite: It *encourages and accelerates* the development of spoken language while reducing the frustration of not being able to communicate verbally.

You can try explaining this to your friend—or just go ahead with what you know is right and not worry about what other people think. Everyone is full of advice on how you should or shouldn't parent your child, but *you* are doing your homework, so you know what's best for *your* baby.

Q. How does signing affect early brain development?

A. Everything your baby experiences from the moment she's born—even as she sleeps—affects the growth and development within her brain. From the feel of soft pajamas against her skin to the sound of your voice, the life and sensory experiences that your little one is exposed to are building the foundation for all future learning.

Your baby is born with billions of brain cells, nearly twice as many as she'll have in adulthood and even many more than she'll have by the age of three. During her first months of life, connecting cells called *synapses* rapidly multiply to the trillions! These cells form pathways between brain cells and act as transmitters throughout the brain, ultimately allowing learning to occur.[2]

If your baby is exposed to more of a particular type of stimulus—in this case, language stimulus—more connections are formed in the language center of her brain. When you have a signed interaction with your baby, she not only receives the message auditorily as with normal speech, but also visually and kinesthetically (physically, through movement or touch), so she's actually receiving the message in triplicate (through three of her senses). When babies consistently receive information in this way, their brains build an extensive network for dealing with language stimulus, and they tend to learn language better and faster. This can conceivably have a long-term effect on all future language-related learning, including picking up foreign languages and reading and writing skills.

So why do we end up with only half of our brain cells by adulthood? It's largely a case of "use it or lose it": The various life and sensory experiences we're exposed to directly affect which brain cells and synapses live or die. Throughout childhood, Mother Nature chisels away the excess cells and synapses in order to make the brain function more efficiently in adulthood.

The first three years of life—*especially the first year*—are the most crucial for building the foundations of language development, and signing with your baby helps make the most of this unique window of opportunity!

Q. Aren't American Sign Language (ASL) signs too hard for babies to make?

A. Babies have limited fine motor coordination, so in the beginning they won't produce the signs exactly as adults do. Just as your baby hears you say the word *water* but first only manages to say "wa-wa," he'll approximate the gestures he sees you make to the best of his ability. He may, for example, clap, bang his fists together, or bring his index finger to his palm in an approximation of the sign **MORE,** rather than managing the precise handshape. Just as you understand when your baby says "wa-wa," you'll also learn to recognize his signed approximations.

Q. My husband and I intend to raise our baby bilingually. When interacting with our child, Daddy speaks English and I speak Spanish. Will the addition of signs confuse our baby?

A. This is an excellent question, and one that comes up often with families attending my classes. The addition of signing will absolutely not confuse your baby. In fact, signing will do just the opposite—it will act as a language bridge, showing your baby that words mean the same thing in both languages. For example, let's say that Mom is offering the baby milk and says *leche* (Spanish for "milk") while making the sign for **MILK.** Later that day, it's Dad's turn to feed the baby. He says *milk* as he signs **MILK.** Because both parents use the same gesture, the baby learns that *milk* and *leche* mean the same thing.

Children who are raised bilingually will often develop spoken language more slowly because they have much more information to process.* Signing can actually help bilingual babies learn both languages better and faster.

Q. Although we live in the U.S., my side of the family is origin- ally from Mexico, and we speak mostly Spanish at home. Is sign language pretty much a universal language, or is it dif- ferent for each country? If so, should we be using Mexican sign language when we speak Spanish to our baby?

---

*Even though children raised bilingually may begin speaking later, this doesn't mean that they're at a disadvantage—quite the contrary. Because bilingual babies are exposed to twice the verbal stimulus, their brains grow more cell connections in the language area of the brain. This results in a lifelong enhanced capacity for language learning.

A. No, there isn't a universal sign language, just as there isn't a universal spoken language. This is because sign languages evolved independently within the deaf communities of each country and/or region. (There was never a "World Sign Language Summit" where all the deaf were able to get together and decide on signs for things and create a universal language.) Contrary to what many people would assume, American Sign Language is *not* "Signed English" (which is something else entirely). ASL is its own independent language and is actually most closely related to French Sign Language.* When choosing which version of sign language to use with your baby, it makes the most sense to go with the one that's in use in the region you live in.

If you live in the U.S., you would use American Sign Language, no matter which spoken languages you use.

*In 1817, Thomas Hopkins Gallaudet and Laurent Clerc, a deaf Frenchman and brilliant teacher, founded the first school for the deaf in the U.S.: The American School for the Deaf in Hartford, Connecticut. This is where the French connection" comes from.

Now that your questions have been answered, you're probably eager to get started signing with your baby! In the following section, we'll discuss *when to start* signing to your baby, *how to sign* to him, and *how to choose first signs* to use.

So turn the page, and let's get started!

part II

getting
started

Aiden's first sign was **MORE** at six months.

Chapter 5

When Can You Start?

You can start signing to your baby at any time, but six to eight months of age is generally considered optimal, since before they're six months old, babies have very little long-term memory to retain the signs they see.

Younger babies also lack the motor skills and hand-eye coordination required to make very precise gestures, so parents may miss their babies' early signing attempts, perceiving them as random gestures. Once they reach six months of age, however, memory retention increases rapidly. If you start signing to your baby when he's between six and seven months of age, for example, you can reasonably expect him to sign back when he's between eight and ten months old. Older babies and toddlers will generally catch on much more quickly because they're reaching the stage in their development when they begin to imitate and attempt to use gestures to communicate. They may take anywhere from a few days to a few weeks to sign back.

Having said this, there's no harm in starting to sign as early as you'd like. It's worthwhile to note that deaf parents sign to their babies from birth, and their children generally sign back significantly earlier than babies in hearing families do. And even among the hearing families I've met and worked with, I've seen a small percentage of babies between four and six months using a sign or two. (In some cases, the parents hadn't even noticed their baby signing until I pointed it out!)

If you're considering starting to sign earlier, just remember that younger babies generally take longer to begin producing signs, so you might not see his first sign for six or seven long months. This delay may cause some parents to become discouraged or even give up. Don't be one of those! Just try to be as consistent as possible and remember that your baby is already gaining many benefits and will begin responding to your signs in other ways long before he signs himself. When you sign **MILK** and your baby goes bananas with excitement or immediately assumes the position and starts rooting around, you understand each other perfectly! One great advantage to starting early is that your baby *could possibly be signing back* by six or seven months of age.

So how do you begin? The next chapter will give you the primer you need.

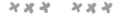

Chapter 6

How to Sign to Your Baby

Signing to your baby isn't the same as just plain talking to her, so it requires some new strategies. It also involves a technique that's different from when you're signing to an adult. In this chapter, we'll discuss methods to get your baby to see your signs, as well as ways to reinforce the meaning of your signs and spoken words.

Get on your baby's level (you should be doing this when you interact with her verbally, too). Get right down on the floor with your child, hold her in your arms or lap, or sit across from her when she's in her high chair. When this isn't possible, slant your sign downward toward her so that she can see it from the intended angle.

Sign in your baby's field of vision. This usually means signing close to your face, just below your line of sight. Babies are naturally attracted to the human face, so they'll be looking in the direction the speech is coming from. "What," you may ask, "do I do if my baby *won't* look at me?" Not to worry, Moms and Dads, we have strategies for handling this in Chapter 9.

Say the word. When signing with hearing babies, it's extremely important to always say the word when you sign it. Ultimately, you want your baby to learn to recognize the spoken word without your signing it, and later to learn to say the word herself. You want to make a strong connection between the spoken word and the gesture.

Sign in context. When your baby is first learning a new sign, she needs to experience the sign *in context* in order to make the association clear to her. For example, don't sign about the bear you saw *yesterday* at the zoo. Instead, sign about the bear *while* you're at the zoo: "Hey! Look at the **BEAR!** What a big, fluffy **BEAR!**" Alternately, you could also sign about a **BEAR** in a book or about a teddy **BEAR.**

Sometimes the context is a feeling such as **PAIN, HOT, COLD, SAD,** or even **MORE.** In these instances, your baby needs to be *feeling* the emotion, sensation, or desire for the connection between word and sign to be clearest. Take the sign **MORE,** for example. Let's say that your baby is just six months old and is primarily still breast- or bottle-fed. You're starting to give her a little rice cereal once a day, and she isn't all that wild about it. You might be excited to start teaching her the sign **MORE** in the context of "more food," but because your baby isn't feeling a keen yearning for more food, she won't make the connection between your **MORE** sign and a feeling (a yearning for more) that she just doesn't have.

Teach motivating signs. Babies want tools to communicate their needs, desires, interests, feelings, and observations. The signs they'll learn most quickly are ones that are the most motivating to them. In the previous example, the baby is just beginning to eat solid foods. But because this particular baby isn't all that excited about eating yet, **EAT** may not be the most motivating sign to teach her at this time. **MILK** would be a better choice, and **MORE** could be taught in the context of **MORE MILK, MORE MUSIC, MORE PLAY,** and so on. (We'll discuss motivating signs more in the next chapter.)

Accompany the sign with the appropriate facial expression. Often the facial expression that accompanies a sign is just as important as the handshape of the sign. For example, the sign for **SCARED** or fearful is accompanied by a startled expression. When parents practice this sign in my classes, however, they often have either a bland or amused expression on their faces. When I stand in front of the class and mirror back to them what this looks like, it usually brings down the house. Try looking in a mirror and practicing the **SCARED** sign with different faces and you'll see what I mean. (The other members of your household will wonder what all that hysterical laughing coming from the bathroom is about!) When you sign to your baby, exaggerating your facial expression makes your meaning much clearer. If your baby laughs at you, all the better—you're making learning fun!

There isn't always an obvious facial expression for a sign, and sometimes there's no specific expression required; while at other times, the expression varies according to the context. For example, what facial expression goes with **MILK?** Well, if you're nursing your baby, you might hold your hand close to your face and sign **MILK** while saying, "Mmm, that's good **MILK!**" You'd probably just instinctively smile at your baby while saying this, since that would be the natural expression for commenting on something being good. If you were offering her milk—as in, "Do you want

MILK?"—you'd want to be sure to really exaggerate the raised eyebrows of your "questioning face" and tone of your voice. When you do this, your baby is not only learning the sign for **MILK,** but she's also grasping another valuable language skill: what a question looks and sounds like. (ASL note: Questions such as "What?" and "Where?" are accompanied by lowered eyebrows, while yes or no questions are accompanied by raised eyebrows.)

Include signing naturally during daily routines and playtime. I can't stress enough how important it is to keep your signing fun and easygoing. If your baby senses that you're stressed out and desperate for his attention, he'll tend to shut you out. It's far better to allow your baby to "absorb" signs naturally, without realizing he's being taught anything.

Let's say, for example, that you're giving your baby a bath. *Water, wash,* and *duck* might be words that pop up frequently at bath time. Here's how *not* to sign with your baby:

> "Look sweetheart, this is **WATER,** okay? When you want **WATER,** do this for Mommy. Sweetie, look at Mommy . . . look here, over here, sweetie! **WATER!**"
>
> (Mom anxiously pleads with her son to look at her signing, but Baby tunes her out—Mommy's game isn't fun.)

Now here's a better idea:

 "Oh my goodness! Look at all this **WATER!** Should we
splash the **WATER?** Look, here comes your **DUCKY!** What
does your **DUCKY** say? Quack! Quack! Can you **WASH** your
DUCKY?"
 (Mom is smiling and relaxed, and so is Baby.)

In the latter example, mother and child are interacting happily
and naturally with each other. Mom engages her child enthusiasti-
cally in what she's talking and signing about, integrating learning
into playing.

By now, you're probably ready to try signing—but which signs
should you use first? The next chapter will help you tackle that
question.

chapter 7

Choosing First Signs

When choosing first signs, our instinct, as parents, is often to select only the ones that express our baby's basic needs. These are usually signs that have to do with daily routines, so let's refer to them simply as *Routine Signs.* While Routine Signs are very important, it is also vital to choose some signs that express your baby's *interests,* thereby *motivating* your little one to try signing. Let's call these *Motivating Signs.*

A good guideline is to start with 3 to 5 each of Routine and Motivating Signs for a total of 6 to 10 signs.

1. Routine Signs: These are signs for things that happen repeatedly throughout the day—signs having to do with daily routines such as **DIAPER, CHANGE, EAT, DRINK,** and so forth. Routine Signs are often the ones that we parents are the most excited (read: *desperate*) for our children to learn, because they're the ones that have the potential to help us more easily meet our babies' basic needs and ward off a lot of crying and whining in the process. Repeating the same signs over and over is good practice for you and your baby and helps you get into the habit of signing. Babies learn best through repetition, and repeating signs helps them make a strong connection between sign, occurrence, and spoken word.

2. Motivating Signs: These are the signs for things that are important to your child and fun for him—that is, things that your baby really loves or gets excited about. Signs for toys, family pets or other animals, cars, babies, music, and so forth make great Motivating Signs. To the parent, these signs often seem less important than Routine Signs, but to your baby, they're actually *much more* *important.* This is because Motivating Signs allow him to communicate things that he can't express by crying and whining!

If your baby is hungry or wet, all he has to do is cry—you'll run through the short list of possible causes and figure out which one it is fairly quickly. Now let's say, for example, that you take your baby for a walk around the neighborhood, and at one point, you visit with a neighbor's cat. The cat is very friendly, and your baby really enjoys seeing and touching it. Later (perhaps even a couple of days later), your baby decides that he'd like to see the cat again or maybe just hear more about cats in general. How can he bring up this topic of conversation? He can cry all he likes, but most likely, neither Mommy nor Daddy will be able to guess "wants cat" as a possible cause of his distress. Using Motivating Signs will teach your baby the power of signing and get him interested in *all* the signs you're showing him.

Clever parents can make Routine Signs into Motivating Signs by integrating them into playtime. If baby just loves his teddy bear, take it and say, "Teddy is hungry. Should we give him something to **EAT?**" or "Teddy needs a **DIAPER CHANGE!**" By incorporating signing with playtime, you can make virtually any sign a Motivating Sign and turn quality time with your child into *super* quality time!

Finally, the day arrives when your child produces his first sign. Once she does, you're over the first hurdle—all of your perseverance has paid off, and you're seeing some concrete proof that your baby is really getting it!

Over the next few weeks, your baby will gradually add more signs. This is an important time because she's still learning to separate all the things in her world into categories, and it takes a while for her to realize that everything has its own distinct sign. For example, not all small animals with four legs are **DOGS**—some are **CATS, RACCOONS,** or **SKUNKS.** Not all liquids are **MILK**—there's also **WATER, JUICE,** and Daddy's **COFFEE;** and each of these have their own signs. As baby adds more signs, this concept will become clearer to her, and one day she'll reach what I call The "Signing Eureka," which appears as a "signing epiphany" of sorts.

Suddenly, your baby will begin signing more often and more spontaneously, sometimes popping up with signs you haven't shown her in weeks. She'll also begin to learn new signs easily, and may even begin to point at things and ask for the sign with a **WHAT?** gesture. My own daughter did this, even though I hadn't intentionally taught her the sign for *what.* I must make that gesture involuntarily a lot!

Other babies may simply point and/or make some kind of vocalization. At this point, the only limit on how many signs your baby can learn is how many you can show her. Just know that parents often find themselves scrambling to keep up with their children's demand for more signs.

Signing with your baby requires more than just learning and using signs—it also demands some creative strategizing on your part. Parents often initially find it difficult to get their baby to "pay attention" and see their signs. Even hearing parents who come from a signing background, such as professional ASL interpreters, are often at a loss as to how to successfully convey signs to their infants. In the following section, we'll discuss how to use signing strategies that are specific to babies and toddlers.

part III

now you're
signing!

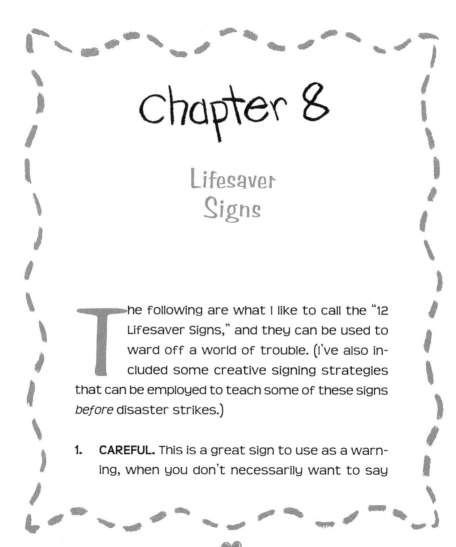

Chapter 8

Lifesaver Signs

The following are what I like to call the "12 Lifesaver Signs," and they can be used to ward off a world of trouble. (I've also included some creative signing strategies that can be employed to teach some of these signs *before* disaster strikes.)

1. **CAREFUL.** This is a great sign to use as a warning, when you don't necessarily want to say

stop—for example, if your child is running but not looking where he's going, or maybe handling something somewhat delicate.

2. **COLD.** A great way to teach this sign is by using a chilled teething ring. Give it to your baby and sign **COLD** repeatedly as she mouths it. In *Sign with your Baby,* author Joseph Garcia recommends using bowls of warm and cold water to teach temperature signs.

3. **GENTLE.** When Baby is pulling the family pet's fur or ears, sign **GENTLE** by stroking her arm and your own in turn.

4. **HELP.** When you notice that your baby is having a hard time with something, ask, "Do you want **HELP?**" and then help her.

5. **HOT.** You can use this sign with things that are only a little bit hot, such as a warm sidewalk or playground equipment in the summer. You can also use it as a warning, paired with **PAIN** and **NO TOUCH** when referring to the stove, barbeque, and so forth. You might even pretend to burn yourself while cooking and sign **HOT** and **PAIN.** With any luck, you'll never get the opportunity to teach this sign in the true context of "burning hot," but if your baby does receive a minor burn, try to remember to sign **HOT** and **PAIN** while you administer first aid and kisses. (Seemingly

minor burns can be very serious for babies and toddlers and often require skin grafts if not treated immediately. If your child burns herself and you have any doubt at all, call the burn unit at your local hospital immediately.)

6. **NO.** Here's a handy sign! Many parents continue to find this sign useful throughout their children's growing years. It's a lot nicer to flash your child a warning **NO** sign than to shout across the room at her, especially in mixed company or places where you need to be quiet, such as in church.

7. **NO TOUCH.** It can be useful to pair **NO** and **TOUCH,** although babies usually know why you're signing just plain **NO** when they're headed for Grandma's glass reindeer collection.

8. **PAIN.** Be sure to use this sign whenever you, your baby, or anyone else is hurting or is wearing a bandage. Always sign **PAIN** at the actual site of the pain so that your baby will learn to localize the sign and be able to show you where it hurts. Sign **PAIN** as an integral part of kissing your child's "boo-boos" better, as a warning about things that can hurt, and to express empathy for someone else who's in pain. (Pretending to bump your head or stub your toe also works here.) For families who aren't accident-prone, teething time provides a great opportunity to use this sign.

9. **SCARED.** If something startles or scares your baby, be sure to use this sign while talking about her fear. Sirena really enjoyed being startled—she'd jump a mile and then laugh with glee when my husband or I would jump out from a corner and say "Boo!" Of course, you don't want to do this unless your baby loves it. You can just wait until something like the Cookie Monster on *Sesame Street* or an alligator at the zoo scares your baby, and then show her the **SCARED** (scary, fear, afraid) sign.

10. **SHARE.** You can use this sign whenever you find yourself mediating between two children who are tussling over a toy, or when you share food with your baby. Break off a piece of your banana and sign **SHARE** before handing your baby a piece. This sign can also be flashed as a warning when you see trouble a-brewin' on the playground.

11. **STOP.** This is a great safety sign. There are a lot of games you can play with the signs **STOP** and **GO** (see Chapter 19), and it's important to try to play games often to teach your baby what these signs mean early on. **STOP** also provides some variety for parents who are tired of saying and signing **NO** all the time.

12. WAIT. There are many times when your baby is fussing over something because he doesn't want to wait. Using this sign at these times will teach your baby that what he wants is coming—but not right this second. I still use this sign a lot with my kids, even though they are three and seven years old and speak perfectly. I find it very useful when I'm on the phone!

Chapter 9

Attention-Getting Strategies

Parents who are skeptical about signing are often concerned that their babies won't pay attention to the signs since their eyes are all over the place and they don't sit still.

If this sounds like your little one, and it probably does, I have some good news: Babies don't need to "pay attention"—at least not as we know it. I once actually saw my daughter learn a sign through her ear. I'm not kidding. (Well, maybe there was some *very* peripheral vision involved, but it didn't seem like it!) Here's what happened.

Sirena and I were enjoying a walk in the park (she was in her stroller) with my friend Cheryl and her baby, when a squirrel ran onto the path. This was my baby's first squirrel, so I quickly signed **SQUIRREL** to her, trying to take advantage of this *in-context teaching opportunity.* I signed again and again, but do you think she would look at me? No way! She was craning her head all over the place trying to see around the bush where the squirrel had run.

Cheryl gave me a bit of a ribbing. "Oh yeah, sure—she's *really* paying attention to you!"

I gave up, and we continued on our walk. About 20 minutes later, another squirrel ran out of the bushes. Sirena turned around in her stroller, looked right at me, and signed **SQUIRREL.**

Cheryl and I were dumbfounded. "She didn't even look at you before!" Cheryl exclaimed.

"I know!" I said. "What did she do, see me sign through her ear?"

The point of the story is this: Don't stress about whether or not your baby is looking at your signs. Signing often—*whether or not your baby is looking at you*—will give you the practice you need to feel comfortable, and you'll also make signing a habit. At the same time, you'll be surprised by how much of your signing your baby actually *does* see, even when he doesn't appear to be paying attention.

There are some great strategies you can use to increase the chances of your child seeing your signs, many of which have been learned by watching deaf mothers interact with their babies. Just as hearing parents raise the pitch of their voices to get their child's attention, deaf parents modify their signing and use various other attention-getting tactics while interacting with their babies.

The following are some great ways to help your baby see your signs:

Verbally get your baby's attention. Call your child's name or use a term of endearment: "Hey, Punkin, look at Daddy!"

Excite the Senses. Oftentimes, babies seem to tune out a parent's voice when they're focused on something else. At times like this, you can use some other sound or sensory stimuli to get your baby's attention.

- *Hearing.* A toy that makes noise or plays music is great for this. Shake a rattle, turn on the music, or roll a noisy toy car along the ground and your baby will most likely turn around to investigate, giving you the perfect opportunity to sign **RATTLE, MUSIC,** or **CAR.**

- *Touching.* Babies are extremely tactile creatures, and they love to experience various sensations. Give your baby a cold teething ring and sign **COLD** as he explores it with his hands and mouth. Use the sensory signs such as **WARM, HOT, COLD,** and **WET** while playing with water of varying temperatures or when showing your baby that playground equipment is too hot, cold, or wet to play on. **WIND** is another sensation that is a great attention getter. Try turning on a **FAN** or taking baby outside on a windy day to use this sign—or show your baby what happens when you blow on a pinwheel.

- *Seeing.* Try using a toy that has movement or flashing lights in order to get your baby's attention.

- *Tasting.* For babies that are ready for it, food can be a terrific motivator for signing! Try using various food or temperature signs at mealtimes. A bowl of **ICE CREAM** makes it very easy to teach signs for **ICE CREAM** and **COLD!**

- *Smelling.* Signing about smells, be they good or bad, is another great way to work in some spontaneous signing with your baby. A crew putting new tar on a road, a freshly mowed lawn, and cookies baking in the oven all provide exciting opportunities for your baby to learn new signs such as **SMELL, STINK, GRASS,** and **COOKIES.**

Seize the moment. Sometimes you and your baby will just look at each other spontaneously, for no particular reason, which is what *Sign with your Baby* author Joseph Garcia terms the "Chance Mutual Gaze."[1] When this happens, you could just grab a nearby toy or other object that might interest your baby, and model the sign for it—for example, "Do you want your **BALL** (or **BOOK** or **BEAR**)?"

Lie in wait. Sometimes the best way to get your baby to look at you is to do nothing at all. If you sit there watching your baby play, he'll look up at you from time to time as if to say, "Are you *still* watching me?" This is the perfect opportunity to sign about whatever it is he's playing with. For example, "You have your **BEAR.** Are you **HUGGING** your **BEAR**?"

Respond to your baby with a sign. Oftentimes throughout the day, your baby will give you a look that says, "I'm trying to tell you something" or "I want information." At moments like these, your baby is actually reaching out to communicate about something specific. This makes it a perfect time to sign. Garcia terms this look the "Expressive Gaze," when your baby wants to express a feeling or ask a question.[2] Let's say, for example, that you're singing a song or playing "This Little Piggie" with your baby, and suddenly, you stop. Your baby would probably look at you in a way that clearly says, "Hey! Why'd you stop?" This is the perfect moment to ask and sign, "Do you want **MORE** singing/piggies?" and then pick up where you left off.

Share experiences spontaneously. Oftentimes, you and your baby will look at the same thing and then at each other. This is known as the "Pointed Gaze,"[3] and once you know about it, you'll notice it happening a lot. Imagine if you went out for a walk with your baby and a crow squawked loudly from the overhead wire. You'd both probably look up at the bird and then at each other, as if to say, "Did you hear that?" This would be an ideal time to say and sign **HEAR** and then point at the bird and say and sign **BIRD.**

Get physical. Videos of deaf mothers interacting with their children show the mothers actively seeking their babies' attention by gently but persistently tapping their hands or other parts of their bodies.[4] Tapping your child's hands when you want him to sign back reminds him that there's something you expect him to do with his hands. You can also stroke or rub him to get his attention—stroking his cheek with a finger, for example, will often get him to turn toward you.

Let your baby see the object and your sign at the same time. At first, you'll find that this is easier said than done. Previously I instructed you to sign close to your face, in your baby's field of vision; however, with babies, these two things don't always go together. Children don't appreciate having their play interrupted and their attention commandeered to learn signs. Smart parents learn to adapt their signing so that their kids can see the sign and the corresponding object while continuing their play.

Here are some strategies to use while playing and interacting with your child:

Sign on your child's body. With some signs, it's just as effective for your baby to feel the sensation of the sign on his body as it is to actually see the sign. The sign for **PET** or **GENTLE** is a great example: If your child is playing with a cat, you could tell him to pet the cat or to be gentle by stroking his arm instead of your own. (Stroking the forearm is the sign for both **PET** and **GENTLE**.) Clearly, your child doesn't need to look at his arm to know what's happening, and his attention is allowed to remain on the cat. Some other signs that work well are **BEAR, COW, DOG,** or **TELEPHONE.**

Put your sign between your child and the object or toy he's interested in. You can either come in from the side or reach around your child with both hands. This works well with signs that only require the use of your hands, such as **BALL, SHOES,** or **MORE.**

Pass objects between yourself and your child. Pick up an object that interests him, bring it toward yourself, produce the sign for it, and then pass it to your child. His eyes will usually track the object long enough for you to produce the sign and pass it back to him. You can pass the object between you like this more than once, signing the name of the object, **PLEASE** and **THANK YOU,** and so on.

chapter 10

Positive Reinforcement

Babies' early attempts at signing are often vague and easy to miss. Parents frequently tell me that they *think* their child may be signing, but they're not sure. If your baby is clapping every time she finishes her food, she's very likely signing her version of the **MORE** sign. (I'll talk more about *approximations* like this in the next chapter.)

When your baby makes any motion that resembles a sign, even if you think it was accidental, be sure to respond as if it were indeed a deliberate sign. It's really important to positively reinforce her efforts. If it wasn't a sign, then nothing's lost; if it *was* an actual attempt to sign, then you've just conveyed a very significant message: What she's doing is right, and you're paying attention to her efforts to communicate.

When your baby is first learning a sign, you should try to reward her efforts whenever possible. If your baby signs **EAT,** try giving her a cracker or a few Cheerios, even if it isn't snack time. If she signs **MILK,** give her a small bottle or nurse her for a few minutes. Children who receive positive reinforcement for their early signing efforts will realize the power of signing more quickly and will attempt to sign more often.

But what happens when your baby's signs don't come out perfectly? That's the topic of our next chapter.

Chapter 11

Signing Mistakes

Young babies and toddlers don't have the motor skills required to make very precise handshapes yet. It's also difficult for them to coordinate two movements at once. Think about all those "baby safe" lids and latches you've installed in your home—even adults have a hard time with some of them! So, because of these factors, your baby will *approximate* many of the signs that she sees you make.

Some commonly used handshapes for babies are:

- An extended index finger
- An open hand with all five fingers extended
- Four fingers extended
- A closed fist

For example, your baby may clap, bang her fists together, or put her index finger to her palm to sign **MORE** rather than producing the precise "flat O" handshape. When using signs with difficult Y handshapes (such as **I LOVE YOU, PLAY,** or **AIRPLANE**), your child may simply use her open hand(s) as if waving.

Your baby may also have trouble coordinating the movement of a sign with its handshape and will often make much bigger movements or leave the movement out entirely. For example, for **FINISHED** or "all done," your baby may wave her entire arms back and forth instead of the smaller flipping-over-the-hands motion. When signing **CAT,** she may just pinch her cheeks, omitting the outward "whisker tracing" movement of the sign.

Because many of your baby's early signing attempts will use these few easier-to-make handshapes, many of her signs will look the same at first. This can be frustrating, but here are some ways you can narrow down her meanings:

- **Location:** Your child may use her open hand to sign **COW** on the side of her head, **AIRPLANE** above her head, **MOMMY** in front of her face, and **I LOVE YOU** to one side of her face. Although the handshape is the same, the location changes the meaning.

- **Movement:** Your baby may use the same handshape but vary the movement, providing an additional clue to her meaning. She may wave both open hands in front of her torso for **PLAY**, bounce the same open hands for **BALL**, and wave her open hands back and forth for **FINISHED** (or "all done").

- **Gaze:** Where is your child looking? She may be looking at what she wants **MORE** of or at the object she's signing about.

- **Context:** Look around and assess the situation; then take a guess. The important thing is that you respond positively to your child's efforts. Even if you don't always get it exactly right, she'll know that you're paying attention and that you're happy and proud she's trying to communicate with you.

When your baby approximates or makes up her own version of a sign, be sure to continue to model the correct sign yourself, as this will give her the repeated opportunity to see the correct version she's striving for. Eventually, her dexterity will improve and her signs will most likely become more like yours. If this doesn't happen, don't worry. *You* know what your baby is telling you, and that's what's really important here.

Using the Wrong Sign

Sometimes children will overgeneralize with signs. For example, your baby may want milk, and she knows that by opening and closing her fists she'll get what she wants, so she'll try the **MILK** sign to get *whatever* she wants. In other words, **MILK** means I **WANT.** (Some children may also use **MORE** to mean "I want.")

When your child overgeneralizes like this, you can take advantage of the opportunity by modeling both the sign she's misusing and a more appropriate sign in the correct context. For example, if your child is signing **MORE** but she really wants food, you can say, "Do you want something to **EAT?**" and give her a few Cheerios. Wait until she's finished eating, and then ask, "Do you want **MORE** Cheerios?"

Sometimes you may think your baby is using the wrong sign, but keep in mind that children see so many things that we adults just don't notice. Once Sirena and I were at an indoor swimming pool and she kept signing **BIRD** to me. I scanned the walls for pictures of birds. Finding none, I told my daughter, "There are no birdies. Birdies are outside."

Sirena was still insistent, nodding her head and signing **BIRD** again. Finally I asked, "Where is the **BIRD?**" She pointed to a gym bag on a bench quite far away. By squinting, I was able make out a tiny label with a picture of a parrot on it. I'd found Sirena's bird.

Sirena also found three kitties (**CAT**) holding up the curtain above Mommy and Daddy's bed. Actually, they're supposed to be clusters of ivy, but now when I lie in bed looking up, I can't see them as anything other than the kitties that Sirena sees.

Another time, my daughter used **MOON** to describe a crescent-shaped dried eucalyptus leaf hanging from a spiderweb on a swing set. Clearly, she knew that the leaf wasn't a moon, but it did look like one: a tiny, shimmering, golden moon, slowly turning on the breeze—a moon that grown-ups couldn't see without the help of a child's eyes.

And just know that sometimes your baby's broad use of signs can make you roll on the ground laughing. One summer our family was staying at a bed-and-breakfast while attending my sister's wedding in Northern California. On the ground floor, there was a very romantic patio restaurant, which Sirena and her daddy were walking through early one evening. As they passed near a table occupied by a voluptuous woman wearing a *very* low-cut blouse, my daughter, who was walking in front of my husband, gave the woman the once-over and then proceeded to sign **MILK** repeatedly as they passed her table. Of course, my husband almost fell on the floor right there. Once they got back to the room, it took him ten minutes before he could stop laughing long enough to tell me what had happened!

chapter 12

Made-Up Signs

While I recommend sticking with ASL signs most of the time, there are some instances when it's more practical to make up a sign. Made-up signs are commonly referred to as "home signs" and are even used in deaf families—although they're generally discontinued by the time children start school.

Maybe you have a Grandma *and* a Nana whom you spend a lot of time with, so you need a different sign for each. You could use **GRANDMA** for one and sign **GRANDMA** + N near your heart for Nana. Or perhaps you have two dogs or three cats. You could opt to sign **DOG** or **CAT** plus an initial to tell them apart. Other times, you'll have an in-context teaching opportunity that you just won't want to miss. Even if you carry a small ASL dictionary around with you, which I strongly recommend, no book has a sign for *everything* in it. For instance, my family lives very close to the world-famous San Diego Zoo and SeaWorld Adventure Park—I take my daughter to both places a lot, and we tend to make up animal signs for the more exotic species, many of which would be finger-spelled in ASL.

Having said all this, I want to caution you against making up too many signs—and when you do, you should record an accurate representation of them that can be understood not only by you, but also by others who care for your child. If you don't do so, you're going to forget the signs you made up . . . but your baby won't. When this happens, you'll really feel stupid—believe me. Sirena would be trying to sign something to me about a recent zoo trip, and for the life of me I wouldn't be able to remember which animal it was. She'd look at me as if to say, "Are you making this up as you go along, or what?" *Oops!* Caught red-handed by my one-year-old!

Babies will also make up their own signs from time to time, which is something that comes naturally to all kids, whether or not they sign. For instance, my daughter made up her own signs for **BLANKET** and **OPEN** (as in, "open a container").

When your baby makes up a sign, you can either opt to keep it and put it into normal use, or you can respond by saying the word and signing the correct ASL version. As with sign approximations, your child's version of the sign will tend to become more like yours as he sees you use your version repeatedly. When deciding whether or not to use a made-up sign, consider what, if any, effect using a made-up sign for that particular item will have in your child's life.

For example, a child who attends a preschool or child-care program where signing is used probably won't run into many problems using a made-up sign for *sea otter,* as sea otters just don't occur all that often in preschool. However, using "home signs" for **TOILET** (potty), **HELP, EAT,** or even **COW** could cause some confusion and frustration at school. Even having a special "pet sign" for that **BLANKET** or **PACIFIER** can cause big problems. It's generally best to stick with actual ASL signs for routine objects and actions, as well as things that are very important to your baby. And deaf or hard-of-hearing children (or children who have deaf or hard-of-hearing family members or close friends) should stick strictly to ASL to limit misunderstanding.

From time to time, parents ask me if it's too late to change a sign to ASL if they've already taught their child a made-up version. In my experience, changing signs later in the game doesn't cause any long-term bewilderment, as babies and toddlers are incredibly adaptable. Just tell and show your baby that you have a new sign for that object or action, and start using the new sign in place of the old one. He'll quickly get the hang of it, just as he does when he makes up a sign and you teach him the correct version or when the whole family uses a "baby talk" word with him and then later switches to the adult version. Of course it's easiest to teach the correct ASL version in the first place whenever possible, so don't underestimate your child's abilities. Older toddlers and preschoolers can even learn to fingerspell simple words!

chapter 13

Setting
Limits

ventually your baby will be happily and en-
thusiastically using signs to get most of
her needs met: When she wants to nurse,
she'll smile at you and sign **MILK;** when she
wants something opened for her, she'll sign **HELP**
before frustration sets in. Most of the time these
exchanges will be free of tears, but what happens
when it's time to cut out that 2 A.M. feeding? While
you do want to reinforce early signing by responding

to your baby's requests, there will come a time when your baby has to learn a harsh truth: *Just because she can <u>sign</u> what she wants doesn't always mean that she'll <u>get</u> what she wants.*

Cutting out Sirena's 2 A.M. feedings nearly broke my heart. I'd go into her room and she'd be standing in her crib desperately signing **MILK.** Eventually this escalated into crying *and* signing, and I did briefly consider that maybe it would have been easier if I could pretend that I didn't know what she wanted. Thankfully, this phase was short-lived, and the benefits far outweighed the heartache.

Once your baby knows a sign for something, it's perfectly reasonable *and necessary* for parents to set limits. If your baby signs **EAT,** for example, you could reply by saying and signing, "I see you're signing **EAT.** We will **EAT** soon. Right now let's look at your **BOOK.**" By responding in this way, you acknowledge your child's request without giving in to it. You're also mirroring back her signs and offering (and signing) an alternative.

Children are going to test for limits, and they'll continue to do so until you show them where the limits are. Signing babies really do want to know if signing will always get them what they want, so using signs such as **SHARE, STOP, GENTLE, NO,** and **SIT** will help teach them boundaries and also give babies a way to express them for themselves. For example, a child who can sign **STOP** or **SHARE** while interacting with other children will be much less likely to resort to hitting or biting. Preschool and child-care programs that use signing find that it dramatically reduces aggressive behavior in the classroom.

While signing with babies does cut down dramatically on the frustration, crying, and tantrums that result from not being able to communicate, it won't completely eliminate the "terrible twos." Your signing toddler will still be likely to throw a screaming tantrum when she doesn't get her way. Nobody's found a cure for that one yet!

chapter 14

Combining Signs

As your baby's signing vocabulary expands, he'll eventually begin combining two or more signs into mini-sentences. This represents a major milestone in your baby's language development and expands his ability to communicate increasingly complex ideas and concepts.

For example, your baby will often combine the sign **MORE** with whatever it is he'd like more of:

MORE + COOKIE or **MORE + MILK.** However, sign combinations such as **HOT + NO + TOUCH** or **BALL + PLAY + DADDY** really take signing to the next level. At this stage, your child is recognizing words and is able to use them in the correct context—all that remains is for his vocal apparatus to catch up, and he'll be off and talking!

As your child begins to talk, he'll also start to combine *spoken* words with signs. He may combine a word he *can* say with the sign for a word he *can't* yet say, such as **BIRD** + "up" or **WHERE** + "Daddy." As your child begins to do this, you may find that he communicates so effectively that you won't remember which words he actually says and which ones he signs!

Your baby will also continue to use signs as needed for clarification or emphasis in the early stages of talking. When he first begins to speak, for example, his spoken versions of *dog* and *doll* may sound a lot alike. Using signs to clarify the meanings of words often helps alleviate a lot of frustration and encourages him to verbalize even more.

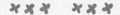

chapter 15

Stumbling
Blocks

As you go along, you may find that some obstacles keep cropping up in your path. This chapter focuses on how to deal with common stumbling blocks in baby sign language.

Starting with Too Few Signs

Parents who start with too few signs may do so out of concern that their child will get confused or "overloaded" by being exposed to too many signs at once. Fear not: *As long as you're consistent* in

signing the words you've chosen, your baby won't become overwhelmed by seeing a lot of signing. As a matter of fact, children who see a lot of signing generally get the hang of it much more quickly.

Once again, you can compare learning to sign with learning to speak. After all, do parents say to each other: "Okay, honey, let's just use these three words around the baby, and when she can say those, we'll add more—we don't want to overload her with

too much talking"? Of course not! You talk and read to your baby as much as possible, and the more you do, the better and faster her language development comes along. Deaf parents sign every word, all the time—and do their children become confused? No. These children actually begin producing signs much earlier than children from hearing families because they learn to sign by total immersion.

When you start with too few signs, you won't sign enough to

become comfortable with signing and make it a habit. Your baby won't get used to looking to you for signing, and he won't have the opportunity to learn signs by seeing you modeling them repeatedly. As we discussed in Chapter 7, choosing three to five signs for things that you frequently see and do each day will ensure that you have signs that can be repeated often during the course of your baby's daily routines.

Starting with Too Many Signs to Be Consistent

Once you realize how fun and easy it is to sign, you may be tempted to start using every sign in this book all at once. However, when you're first starting out, it's wise not to bite off more than you can chew. Try beginning with about 6 to 10 signs, and then gradually add more as you feel ready, using as many as you can comfortably remember to sign consistently. The more consistent you are with the signs you are using, the more quickly your baby will begin to make the connection between those signs and the things they represent.

What might your baby be thinking if you only occasionally produce the **MILK** sign when you nurse? *What's Mommy doing with her hand?* she might wonder. *Is it something to do with milk? No, that can't be it—she didn't do that the last time I nursed.*

Your baby will make the connection more easily when you sign consistently. Of course nobody remembers to sign *every* time—not even me—so don't beat yourself up if you forget to sign. Your baby will catch on eventually, even if you're a little flaky with the signing.

Overanticipating Baby's Needs

Because you can often tell what your baby wants, even without signing, you may tend to overanticipate her needs. You can see that the pile of Cheerios on her high chair's tray has run out and that she's starting to whine a little—clearly she wants **MORE**. Because you want to prevent the situation from escalating into crying, you're likely to rush in immediately with more cereal. But if you've been working on the **MORE** sign with your baby, you can first try to give her some hints and encouragement as to how she can more effectively get her needs met.

For example, ask your baby, "**WHAT** do you want? Can you show me with your hands?" (Tap her hands.) "Do you want **MORE?**" (Sign **MORE.**) Then give her more Cheerios, whether or not she's responded to your efforts. You can also try to mold her hand into the shape of the sign if she'll let you—but you should stop if this seems to annoy her at all, as you want to keep this fun and lighthearted.

Not Using Motivating Signs

I can't stress enough how important it is to use signs that are motivating to your baby. If she doesn't feel a strong need or desire to communicate something, she'll be much less likely to use the sign for it. The signs your baby will use most quickly are the ones that she's absolutely *desperate* to communicate. (For more on this, please refer back to Chapter 7.)

Sirena enjoys signing a story with her cousin Ruby and Aunt Susan.

chapter 16

Including Caregivers, Family, and Friends

Anyone who cares for or regularly interacts with your child can and should be involved in signing with him. The more you can get family members, friends, and caregivers in on it, the better your baby's signing will come along.

Signing with Family Members

Sometimes parents run into resistance from other family members. A misinformed but well-meaning grandparent may be concerned that a signing child who can just use his hands will become "too lazy" to talk, for instance, or a spouse may mistakenly believe that signing will stigmatize the child as "slow" or disabled. Some dads may not take the idea of baby sign language seriously or may consider it as something that's in "Mom's department."

It can often be difficult to get these people to read a book when they already have a negative or passive mind-set, so a really great way to win them over is to bring them to a baby sign language class or show them an instructional video that includes babies actually signing.

Even skeptical family members will most likely be won over once they see your baby actually start to sign—they won't be able to resist having that kind of close, communicative relationship with him, too.

Signing and Siblings

Whether or not you've ever signed with your older child, big brothers and sisters love learning signs and teaching them to a new baby. It's a great way for an older child to interact with the baby, who may still be too young to "play," and babies tend to be especially fascinated by everything an older child does. Helping to teach a younger sibling to sign is an important job for a big sister or brother and is something they can be very proud of! They can sign during playtime or while Mommy or Daddy's hands are full with changing, feeding, or driving the car. Preschool-age siblings can even "read" a story to the baby by signing about the pictures in a book, while elementary-age children can read aloud as they sign the words. And signing is still *extremely beneficial* to older children. Even after children can talk, signing continues to enhance literacy skills, improving vocabulary, spelling, and reading. So, if having a new baby in the house gets your older ones interested in signing, all the better!

Signing and Child Care

Many working parents would love to sign with their babies, but they're concerned about how signing will fit into the child-care picture. If your little one will be spending most of his day in someone else's care, then the other caregiver(s) should most definitely be involved in his signing program as well.

Many child-care and preschool programs are starting to include signing as an integral part of their curriculum. Early childhood educators who keep up on current research in the field of child development know that signing with the children in their care not only makes life easier and happier for the kids, but it's also easier and happier for the staff. In fact, I'm regularly asked to speak to large groups of early-childhood professionals and educators, and I frequently teach private classes for parents and staff at day-care and preschool programs.

When searching for a child-care provider or a preschool for your child, start looking early and ask each program director if any signing is used with the children who attend their facility. If the answer is no, ask if they'd be willing to learn and use certain signs with your child. If they've never heard of signing with hearing children, you could explain the benefits, lend them this book, tell them about any classes in your area, or even ask if they'd be willing to watch a DVD (if you have one).

Occasionally, you're going to run across child-care providers or program directors who are resistant or even hostile to the idea of signing with babies, usually because they're either misinformed or uneducated about the topic. If you run into a situation where the person in charge isn't receptive to the idea of signing with babies, cross this place off your list of possible child-care providers. In my view, they don't have the best interests of children at heart. The benefits of signing with babies are clearly proven, but sometimes you can't teach an old dog new tricks. Some administrators just get so mired in the paperwork end of things that they don't keep up with the latest research and developments in early-childhood education . . . nor do they have any interest in doing so.

Nannies are a great option if you can afford one. Younger nannies and au pairs are often enthusiastic, receptive to new ideas, and eager to expand their credentials with more education; and older, more experienced nannies have done enough hands-on child rearing to really understand the benefits of signing. As a matter of fact, when I have an information table or booth at a baby store or family event, the people who approach my table most often are older parents and adoptive or foster parents (who are often more mature), as well as grandparents. These people have been around children long enough to really understand the potential benefits that signing offers.

When you interview a nanny or babysitter, arrange some time to explain your child's signing program in detail, showing some video or getting your baby to demonstrate, if possible. Mark the signs your child uses right in this book so that the caregiver can reference them easily. You might even consider copying and posting a few of the pictures from this book in relevant areas—for example, mealtime signs near the high chair. The Sign2Me™ online store offers special laminated posters just for this purpose, in various signing themes.[1]

Signing with Friends and Peers

Parents often ask me if young babies will actually sign to each other. Sirena and I were members of the same playgroup from the time she was only a few weeks old. Most of the babies were born within a few months of each other, and like me, many of the mothers signed with their babies.

Initially, we'd looked forward to sitting around the playground, watching our babies carry on conversations with their little hands. As we've since learned, babies aren't all that interested in interacting with each other. When they play, they engage in *parallel play,* which means that they'll play *next to* each other rather than actively *with* each other. Little babies are actually far more interested in interacting with adults. Maybe this is nature's way of avoiding the "blind leading the blind," so to speak. Whatever the reason, don't expect a lot of signing between younger babies.

On occasion, however, the other parents and I *have* witnessed a few signed interactions between our babies. When Sirena was still too young to walk, for instance, another mother and I saw my daughter signing **MILK** to her son. Both of us moms were still nursing, so we found this really amusing. What was Sirena doing—recommending my milk to another baby? "Hey, you should try my mom's milk. It's the best!"

As the little ones in our group moved from babyhood to toddlerhood, we noticed them signing to each other more. Some learned to sign **SHARE,** for example, instead of just grabbing toys from their playmates. They sometimes signed interactions about the toys they were playing with or the experiences they were sharing. In addition, many of the mothers prompted their kids to use **PLEASE, SORRY,** and **THANK YOU** with the other children (and adults) when appropriate.

When Sirena first started using signs with other children, I worried that her feelings would be hurt if she signed to a child who didn't know how to sign back. I felt bad for her when she walked up to another child and signed **PLAY,** only to get a blank stare in return. Once she was a talker, however, I realize that this is just how toddlers and preschoolers often are—they don't have all the social graces in place yet. Sirena would walk up to a child she didn't know and *say,* "My name is Sirena. Do you want to play?" More often than not, she would still get the same blank stare in response.

This leads to the inevitable question: What happens to signing after your child starts to speak? That's what the next chapter is all about.

Sirena, age three, signs **MORE.**

Chapter 17

Is There Signing After Talking?

"Will my baby continue to sign after she can talk?" is a common question parents ask in my classes. In general, babies will use the tools they have for as long as they need them. As children begin to speak, there's a short period of "overlap" when they simultaneously say *and* sign certain words.

A baby who knows how to sign **MORE,** for example, will use that sign for preverbal communication

and will likely continue to use it as she begins to attempt to verbalize the word *more.* She'll keep signing to clarify the meaning of the spoken word until she knows that you can understand her easily. Eventually your baby will drop the sign for **MORE,** but she may still use it for emphasis on occasion.

For example, sometimes I'd be washing dishes or be otherwise occupied, and my daughter would announce: "I want more juice, Mommy!"

If I didn't whip my gloves off right away and get her the juice (which there's no way I'd do), Sirena would put her hands in front of my face and repeatedly say *and* sign **MORE,** as if to communicate, "Maybe you can't hear me, so let me spell it out for you: I want **MORE!**"

Some parents have high hopes that their children will continue to sign as a second language, but children will do what their parents, and later their peers, do. If you continue to sign *and* talk, then your baby might do the same for a time. Most hearing parents, however, tend to drop the signs as soon as their babies learn them, and their babies drop the signs as they begin to talk.

Toddlers can be taught to continue to use signs with deaf or hard-of-hearing family members if they spend enough time with them. Just as babies in bilingual households can learn that they must always use Spanish with Grandpa, signing children will use the tools they have to communicate when they need to.

Sometimes parents who have begun signing with their older toddlers want to introduce signs for words that their children can already say. In my experience, toddlers who can talk won't use signs for words that they can already say well. Because it's easier to simply say the word, they have no motivation to sign it. (Children of all ages, however, enjoy using signs along with songs, even with words they can say.)

Many hearing families continue to find signing useful long after their children can speak, and there are many situations where signing may actually be preferable to talking. For example, parents can flash I **LOVE YOU** across the track, playing field, or pool when their child performs well in a sporting event. (The vast majority of older kids and teens prefer this approach to Mom standing in the bleachers screaming, "Mommy loves you, sweetie!") In addition, a parent or child can sign **TOILET** (potty) in mixed company without risking embarrassment. I often sign **WAIT, QUIET, SIT,** or **STOP** to my children if they're trying to interrupt when an adult is speaking or if we're in a place where we need to be quiet, such as a library or in church. My husband will sign things to me across a crowded room.

When I wrote the first edition of *Baby Sign Language Basics* in 2003, Sirena was only three years old. Already, she was talking a mile a minute and could say just about anything, although I'd occasionally catch her signing with her dolls or stuffed animals, and she still enjoyed signing along with songs and games.

Today, Sirena is eight years old. Her teachers and other adults often comment on her advanced vocabulary and how well she speaks. She now has a little brother—Aiden, age four. We all signed with him, too, and like his sister, he's an advanced talker. Parents at the playground sometimes ask me how old he is, and they're surprised by his excellent vocabulary, especially when compared with other little boys of this age who are often not so verbal. I always tell people that I signed with my kids, and I truly believe that signing gave them a tremendous boost in their verbal development.

I'm also constantly amazed by how many signs both children still remember, and occasionally use. I'd love my children to have the opportunity to learn ASL as a second language. They already have such a great head start in this valuable skill.

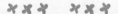

Chapter 18

The Greatest Gift

When all is said (or *signed*) and done, the greatest benefit of signing with your baby isn't increased IQ, enhanced language development, or the ability to meet his needs more quickly and with less crying. In my opinion, the greatest benefits of signing are emotional: allowing open communication and mutual understanding, and deepening the bonds of love and trust between parent and child like nothing else.

Children who learn to sign early on quickly realize that they're loved and valued members of the family, whose thoughts and ideas are important. Is there any better message you can give your baby than that?

Each sign you give your child is a precious gift, one that will be returned to you over and over. As your baby begins sharing his impressions of the world with you, you'll discover an exciting new place together, vibrant with color and imagination—in other words, the world seen through *his* eyes.

No parent and child should miss out on this once-in-a-lifetime opportunity. However, signing with hearing babies is still a fairly new idea, and as of this writing, many people haven't heard of it yet. Eventually, baby sign language classes will be as commonplace as childbirth classes, and many hospitals already do offer baby sign language as part of their women's health curriculum. Please help spread the word by sharing the gift of baby sign language with the parents and caregivers in your life.

And now, let's really have some fun with what we've learned! Part IV will help you and your baby have a blast with your favorite signs.

part IV

signing
for fun

Chapter 19

Signing and Playing

Playtime provides a wonderful opportunity to make signing fun and engaging for you and your baby. You can integrate signs into just about any kind of game or activity—the following are just a few suggestions. Enjoy!

- **Hide-and-Seek with Toys:** Place a toy partially under a blanket or behind your back. (Animal toys are good, as babies love animal signs!) Ask where the toy is—signing **WHERE**—and then ask, "Can you find the **COW?**" or whatever it is you hid.

- **Hide-and-Seek with People:** Have one parent hide while baby and the other parent "seek." Sign and ask, "**WHERE** is **DADDY** (or **MOMMY**)?" Then add silliness and suspense by looking in ridiculous places, such as under rugs and in small drawers, before actually finding the person hiding.

- **Light On/Light Off:** Point out the **LIGHT** to your baby. Turn it on, signing **LIGHT ON,** and then turn it off and sign **LIGHT OFF.** This is a big favorite! You can also play this game with a fan, signing **FAN, STOP,** and **MORE.**

- **Dance to the Music:** Ask your baby, "Do you want **MUSIC?**" Turn on the CD player or a music box and sign **MUSIC.** Then ask, "Do you want to **DANCE?**" Pick your little one up and dance around the room. Turn off the music, putting baby down and telling her the music **STOPPED.** Then ask if she wants **MORE** and do it all again!

- **Mirror Play:** This is a simple game that's very popular with babies. Sit in front of a mirror with your baby in your lap. Talk about yourself and your baby, your facial expressions and emotions, your body parts, your clothing, or his toys. You could sign **HAPPY**, **CRYING**, **I LOVE YOU,** or "**WHERE** is your nose?" (Sign his body parts by circling them with your finger.)

- **Guessing Game:** Sign and talk about pictures in a book and have baby find and point to them. For example, sign "**WHERE** is the **ELEPHANT?**" and then let baby find the picture of the elephant on the page.

- **Shoe Game:** You can play this game anywhere, anytime! Put your hands or fingers inside a pair of your baby's shoes and hit the shoes together. Sign **SHOES** and then show them **WALKING, RUNNING, JUMPING,** and **DANCING**—making the signs after the shoes perform each action.

- **Simon Says:** This is a great toddler game. One parent can be "Simon" and say and sign commands such as **WALK, RUN, JUMP, STOP,** or **GO,** while the other parent and baby follow directions.

- **Doll Signs:** Sign to and about your child's favorite dolls or stuffed animals. This is a terrific way to make routine signs more motivating, since a child who doesn't show much interest in learning the **DIAPER CHANGE** sign might be engaged by performing this mundane task on his favorite teddy bear. Say and sign, "**BEAR** needs a **DIAPER CHANGE!**"

- **Let's Pretend!:** Play "house," "store," or "fire station" with your child; and sign about the different things you're doing. A favorite game invented by my daughter was "buy new": We'd take shopping bags and "shop" for various items around the house, signing the items as we put them into bags. We also bartered between our bags for each other's purchases.

- **Dress-Up Box:** Use signs to comment about the clothes, such as **HAT, DRESS, SHOES,** or **BEAUTIFUL.**

Aiden signs that the bunny is sleeping.

Chapter 20

Storytime

Signing along with books makes reading more fun and interactive for your baby and provides an opportunity to sign about things that are out of the realm of her day-to-day experiences. Combining pictures with vocabulary and signs reinforces new ideas for your baby and gives her a way to actively participate by commenting on the story and pictures.

When you read a story together, even when you're not signing, try to sit with your baby propped up across from you—"storytime at the library" style. This will allow her to watch your facial expressions and/or signs, and it also lets you see her reaction as you tell the story, which is a lot more fun than looking at the back of her head (even though the backs of babies' heads *are* very cute!).

When you read to your baby, remember that you don't have to read the entire story or even tell the *same* story that the author's telling. Babies have short attention spans, so pointing at the pictures (or letting your baby do the pointing) and talking about what you see generally works better than trying to follow the text word for word.

You can use signs with most picture books, but there are a few types that lend themselves especially well to signing and reading:

1. Books with one concept per page. Having only one concept per page makes it very clear to your baby what you're signing about. *Brown Bear, Brown Bear, What Do You See?* by Bill Martin, Jr., and illustrated by Eric Carle is a great example of this type of book.

2. Books that repeat the same concept on each page. This type of book gives you the opportunity to reinforce one sign through repetition. *Goodnight Moon* and *The Runaway Bunny* by Margaret Wise Brown and illustrated by Clement Hurd are good examples. Both books have bunnies on most pages, and *Goodnight Moon* has a mouse hiding on each page, too!

3. Vocabulary-building books with pictures of many objects on each page. These books are great for signed and verbal vocabulary building. You can also play a "let's find" game by signing an object and asking your child to find it on the page. There are many of these books available, such as *Baby's Book of Animals* by Roger Priddy or *Richard Scarry's Best Word Book Ever.*

ASL books created especially for children are also available. You can find them online or at your local library or bookstore. They're wonderful because they often show pictures of children signing, are based on subjects of special interest to children, and include signs along with the pictures on each page. For a list of children's signing books, see the Resources section at the back of this book.

You don't have to limit yourself to just reading children's books with your baby—any book or magazine with engaging pictures will do. Find photographs of babies and children in parenting magazines, food layouts in gourmet magazines, and wildlife photos in *National Geographic* (but screen the content first for scary pictures!). Magazines for cat, dog, horse, boat, and car lovers are also terrific for showing many versions of the same thing. Are Chihuahuas and Great Danes really both dogs? Leafing through a copy of *Dog Fancy* magazine is a good way to show just how many different kinds of **DOGS** there are.

And reading isn't the only fun way to use your signs—there are plenty of nursery rhymes and songs that are great to sign along with. Turn the page and you'll see what I mean!

chapter 21

Sing, Sign, and Rhyme!

Old McDonald
(Sign along with the animal name and sound!)

Old McDonald had a farm
E -I- E- I- O!
And on that farm he had a **COW**
E -I- E- I- O!
With a moo moo **[COW]** here
And a moo moo **[COW]** there

Here a moo [**COW**]
There a moo [**COW**]
Everywhere a moo moo [**COW**]
Old McDonald had a farm
E -I -E -I -O!

(Repeat with **HORSE**, chicken [**BIRD**], **PIG, CAT, DOG,** and so on.)

The Wheels on the Bus

The wheels on the **BUS** go round and round
[circle fists round and round each other]
Round and round, round and round
The wheels on the **BUS** go round and round
All through the town

The **BABIES** on the **BUS** say, "I want **MILK,**
I want **MILK,** I want **MILK**"
The **BABIES** on the **BUS** say, "I want **MILK**"
All through the town

The **MOMMIES** on the **BUS** say, "**I LOVE YOU,**
I LOVE YOU, I LOVE YOU"
The **MOMMIES** on the **BUS** say, "**I LOVE YOU**"
All through the town

Are You Sleeping

Are you **SLEEPING,** are you **SLEEPING**
BABY of mine, **BABY** of mine?
BABY likes to **SLEEP, BABY** likes to **SLEEP**
Let's **SLEEP MORE,** let's **SLEEP MORE**

Are you **EATING,** are you **EATING**
BABY of mine, **BABY** of mine?
BABY likes to **EAT, BABY** likes to **EAT**
Let's **EAT MORE,** let's eat **MORE**

(Repeat with other verbs such as **WALKING,**
SINGING [MUSIC], DANCING, SWINGING, or **PLAYING.**)

I've Got the Whole World

I've got a bouncy **BALL** in my hands
I've got a bouncy **BALL** in my hands
I've got a bouncy **BALL** in my hands
I've got a **BALL** in my hands

I've got a fluffy teddy **BEAR** in my hands
I've got a fluffy teddy **BEAR** in my hands
I've got a fluffy teddy **BEAR** in my hands
I've got a teddy **BEAR** in my hands

I've got a yummy **BANANA** in my hands
I've got a yummy **BANANA** in my hands
I've got a yummy **BANANA** in my hands
I've got a **BANANA** in my hands

I've got **MOMMY'S KEYS** in my hands
I've got **MOMMY'S KEYS** in my hands
I've got **MOMMY'S KEYS** in my hands
I've got her **KEYS** in my hands

(Feel free to substitute other signs, such as yummy **COOKIE**
or **GRANDMA'S** phone [**TELEPHONE**]**,** and so forth.)

118

FIVE little **MONKEYS**

Jumping on the **BED**

ONE fell off and bumped his head **[PAIN** at head]

MOMMY called **[TELEPHONE]** the doctor

And the doctor said:

"**NO MORE MONKEYS**

JUMPING on the **BED!**"

Five Little Ducks

FIVE little **DUCKS** went out to **PLAY**
Over the hills and far away
MOMMY DUCK said, "Quack, quack, quack"
And **FOUR** little **DUCKS** came waddling back

FOUR little **DUCKS** went out to **PLAY**
Over the hills and far away
MOMMY DUCK said, "Quack, quack, quack"
And **THREE** little **DUCKS** came waddling back
[Repeat with three, two, one, and no ducks.]

MOMMY DUCK went far away
Looking for her **BABIES** who'd gone to **PLAY**
DADDY DUCK said, "Quack, quack, quack"
And **MOMMY** and **BABIES** came waddling back

✖ ✖ ✖

The More We Get Together

The **MORE** we **SIGN** together, together, together
The **MORE** we **SIGN** together, the **HAPPIER** we'll be
For your **FRIENDS** are my **FRIENDS**
And my **FRIENDS** are your **FRIENDS**
The **MORE** we **SIGN** together, the **HAPPIER** we'll be

(Repeat with **SIGN [MUSIC], PLAY, HUG, DANCE,** and **JUMP.**)

Three Nice Mice

THREE nice **MICE, THREE** nice **MICE**
See how they **PLAY,** see how they **PLAY**
They're always polite when they nibble **[EAT]** their cheese
They always remember to say **THANK YOU** and **PLEASE**
They cover their noses [finger circles nose] whenever they
sneeze [mime sneezing]
THREE nice **MICE**

If You're Happy and You Know It

If you're **HAPPY** and you know it, clap your hands
If you're **HAPPY** and you know it, clap your hands
If you're **HAPPY** and you know it
Then your **FACE** [index finger circles face] will surely show it
If you're **HAPPY** and you know it, clap your hands

(Repeat with different fun signs and actions. This song combines signs **[HAPPY, FACE, HOORAY]** and actions [clap your hands, jump, blow a kiss] and is great for burning off some extra toddler energy!)

appendix

Signing Vocabulary

The following section contains more than 300 signs for use with babies and toddlers, listed alphabetically.

When you're ready for more signs or need one that isn't included here, you can refer to ASL dictionaries, which are available in the languages section at bookstores, online, and at your local library. Another wonderful resource is Michigan State University's ASL Browser Website,

www.commtechlab.msu.edu/sites/aslweb, which shows a Quick-Time video clip of the sign you're looking for. If you have Internet access, using this site is a great way to make sure that you've interpreted the signs you find in print correctly. With some signs, it can be difficult to determine the movement portion of the sign from a still picture (even if they have directional arrows), so watching a video of signs being produced can be very helpful.

In my descriptions of each sign, I sometimes refer to an *action hand* and a *base hand.* The action hand is the one that performs the primary movement portion of the sign, while the base hand remains stationary or moves less. The action hand should be your dominant hand—that is, the right hand for "righties" and the left hand for "lefties." With one-handed signs, "lefties" will sign with their left hand, and "righties" will sign with their right. Sometimes I may refer to the right or left hand in my descriptions. In these cases, lefties should simply reverse the hands. If you use your nondominant hand to do the dominant action of a sign, it will feel awkward, so that's a clue to switch hands.

Parents often ask me if their baby will be confused if different caregivers use different hands to sign, but you don't need to worry about that at all. Babies are pretty much ambidextrous, and they'll use their right and left hands interchangeably. They'll just assume that you're doing the same.

The Manual Alphabet

Don't freak out on me now—I'm not expecting you to start finger spelling to your baby! Your baby is too little to learn to spell yet, and although she'll be able to form some of the letters before she can talk, she probably won't have the coordination to do others correctly until at least age three.

I've included this manual alphabet for a couple of reasons. First, sometimes I use terminology relating to the manual alphabet when describing signs. For example, I may tell you that the sign for **PLAY** is made by shaking the "Y" hands, or that the sign for **TOILET** is made by shaking the "T" hand. I always strive to describe the handshapes in the simplest possible terms, and using the manual alphabet letter is oftentimes the clearest way. As you look at the photos of the signs and read the descriptions, you'll naturally begin to learn how some of the letters are formed.

Another reason why I've included the manual alphabet is that many parents have asked me if there's a way to make up a sign for their child's name or the names of other family members, friends, or pets.

In the deaf community, name signs are traditionally given by a deaf person and often incorporate the first letter of the person's name and some physical or personality attribute of whoever's being named.

The deaf create name signs as a way of identifying other people within their community, and most people within the deaf community are adamant that these kinds of signs only be given by a deaf individual.

If you aren't lucky enough to have a deaf friend or family member around to bestow this honor upon you, there *is* an accepted way to make up a "name indicator." Simply sign the first letter of the person's name over your heart. If it's Grandma Barbara, for example, you can sign **GRANDMA** and then the sign for *B* over your heart.

Keep in mind that this isn't a "name sign." You're simply referring to the person by their initials, which is something we do in spoken language as well, for example, like calling someone J. D. or Aunt B.

The Manual Alphabet

A B C D

E F G H

I J K L

M N O P

Q R S T

U V W

X Y Z

ASL Numbers

The following chart shows ASL numbers from one to ten. Using number signs with counting games and songs is a great way to introduce "pre-math" concepts to babies, toddlers, and preschoolers. As with the ASL alphabet, learning ASL numbers also helps with understanding handshapes used in other signs.

ASL Numbers 1–10

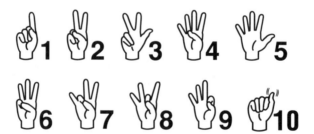

Again

The fingertips of the curved action hand come down in an arc to touch the upturned palm of the base hand.

Airplane

The "Y" hand, with the index finger extended and palm down, moves up and away from the body, representing the wings and fuselage of an airplane flying through the sky.

Alligator

The fingers of both hands bend at the knuckles, forming "claw hands." The hands open and close on each other, like an alligator's jaws snapping open and shut.

Ambulance/Siren

The "5" hands are raised with fingers bent, and rotate from side to side like lights on an ambulance.

Angry

The fingers pull down and away from the forehead, to show how the face wrinkles when angry.

Animal

The fingertips of both hands rest on the chest as the hands move back and forth toward each other. This represents the animal's breathing.

Ape

Thump your chest with
both fists, like a gorilla.

Apple

The knuckle of the bent index finger twists on the cheek near the corner of the mouth, representing the stem being twisted out of an apple.

Aunt

The "A" handshape circles near the chin. Female signs are always done near the chin/jaw area.

Baby

One arm cradles the other and
rocks side to side, as if rocking
a baby.

Babysitter/Nanny

Use the sign for "keep": Rest one "K" hand on top of the other at an angle. The letter K is signed by holding up the first two fingers with the middle finger slanted in at an angle. Now, move both hands in a small circle in front of you. This changes the meaning to "care."

Bad

 The flat hand touches the mouth as if tasting something, and then turns it away, palm down, because it's bad.

Ball

The curved hands, with fingers spread, bounce toward each other, as if holding a ball.

Balloon

The hands outline a balloon
that is being blown up.

Banana

Go through the motions of peeling a banana. The extended index finger of the base hand represents the banana while the fingertips of the action hand pull down the skin.

Bath

The closed fists scrub up and down the body.

Bear

The two "claw hands" are crossed over the chest and make scratching motions, like a bear scratching itself.

Beautiful

 The open hand starts on one side of the face and swoops up and around, closing as it reaches the chin.

Bed

(Although there is a separate sign for *sleep,* you can use this sign for *sleep, nap,* and *rest,* too.) Rest your head on your hand, as if it's a pillow.

Bee

 The "F" handshape touches the cheek, representing a bee stinging, and then the flat hand brushes it away.

Bell

The right hand is held facing down with the wrist bent and fingertips and thumb close together, representing a bell shape. The "bell" strikes the open left hand twice.

Big

The side-held hands move away from each other, showing the large size of something. Note the extended, bent fore-fingers and raised thumbs.

Bike

The hands go through the
motions of pedaling a bicycle.

Bird

The index finger and thumb
are held close to the mouth and
open and close like a bird's beak.

Bite

One hand bites the other hand.

Black

The tip of the index finger is drawn across the forehead, indicating black eyebrows.

Blanket

 The downturned hands grasp
and pull up and imaginary blanket.

Blue

Make a "B" hand-shape by holding up your flat hand with your fingers together and your thumb bent in-ward across your palm. Shake your "B" in the space off the right shoulder. (This is the area where some color signs are made.)

Boat

Cup your hands together to make a little "boat" and make it move away from you with a rolling motion, like a boat moving through the water.

Book

Hold hands flat with palms together. Open hands like the covers of a book.

Boy

 The hand grasps the brim of a cap. Male signs are always done in the forehead/temple area.

Bread

The flat base hand represents a loaf of bread, which is then sliced a couple of times by the fingertips of the action hand.

Broken/Break

The fists go through the motions of breaking a stick.

Brother

 With both index fingers extended, tap the forehead with the right hand, then bring it down on top of the opposite hand. Male signs are always done in the forehead/temple area.

Brown

The "B" hand moves down
the side of the right cheek.

Brush Hair

Mimic the act of holding the handle of a brush and brushing hair.

Bubbles

There are two different ways to sign bubbles.

1. The cupped hands mimic catching bubbles and popping them.

2. The "F" hands alternately rise up, like bubbles in the air.

Bug/Insect

Touch your thumb to your nose as you wiggle your first two fingers. This represents an insect wiggling its antenna around.

Build

 The hands show things being
stacked on top of each other.

Bus

ASL version

Non-ASL version

ASL version

Pull an imaginary cord with your bent first two fingers. This is a fun but lesser-known sign. It's used in the *Signing Time!* videos, which I love.

Non-ASL version

The two fists mimic steering a large, low-down steering wheel. This is similar to **CAR,** but with the fists held horizontally on a bigger steering wheel. *Bus* is most commonly finger spelled in ASL, so this isn't an official ASL sign.

Butterfly

The hands fly around with the thumbs locked against each and the fingers wiggling, representing a butterfly flying.

Cake

The action hand, with fingers bent into a "claw," rises up from the palm of the base hand, showing how a cake rises.

Camera

Pretend to look through a
camera and push the but-
ton to take a picture.

Candle

The index finger of one hand represents the wick, while the wiggling fingers of the opposite "5" hand represent a flame.

Candy

The tip of the index finger is twisted on the cheek.

Car/Drive

Both hands move in opposite arc motions, grasping an imaginary steering wheel.

Careful

Stack one "K" hand on top of the other "K" hand and rotate them forward in a circle like a wheel turning. Be sure to make a concerned facial expression.

Cat

The thumb and index finger come together at the upper lip and move outward and away from the face as if sliding whiskers through the fingers. Can use one or both hands.

Catch (a ball)

The hands mimic catching a ball.

Catch (grab, capture)

Both hands, palms down with the right over the left, quickly close into "S" hands.

Cereal

 Bend and straighten the index finger as it moves from right to left across the chin—like wiping away milk from the chin.

Change

 The two fists are held together, facing opposite directions, with knuckles touching. Both hands pivot in opposite directions to change places.

Chase

The action "A" hand makes a spiraling motion as it chases the opposite "A" hand, which moves away in a smooth motion.

Cheese

 The heel of the downturned right hand presses against the heel of the upturned left hand as they rotate back and forth against each other.

Child/Children

Pretend to pat the head of
an imaginary child (or children).

Christmas

The "C" hand outlines the shape of a wreath.

Clean
(adjective, as in "not dirty")

The downturned hand wipes dirt off of the opposite upturned hand in one smooth motion. (This is also used for **NICE.**)

Clean
Clean up/Wash (verb)

The closed fist scrubs the opposite open palm in a circular motion, as if washing something.

Climb

The hands go through the
motions of climbing a ladder.

Close

The "B" hands come together, facing out, to show that something is closed.

Clouds

The open hands are held up and turn inward,
repeatedly outlining the puffy shape of clouds.

Coffee

Stack one fist over the other, moving the top fist in a circular motion as if grinding coffee. (Yes, I know babies don't drink coffee, but they're very interested in yours!)

Cold

The shoulders are hunched and the clenched hands shake, as if shivering with cold.

Color

The fingers wiggle in front of the mouth.

Comb Hair

Comb hair with fingers.

Come

This is a natural gesture. Beckon your child by moving your palm toward your body while slightly bending the fingers. Another version is to beckon with one or both index fingers.

Cook

 The flat action hand lays on the flat base hand and then quickly flips over, like flipping a pancake to cook the other side.

Cookie

 This sign mimics cutting out a cookie with a cookie cutter. The action hand is held in a "claw" shape and twists around and back again against the opposite flat palm, as if cutting through dough.

Corn

The hands twist the ends of an imaginary cob of corn near the mouth.

Cow

The thumb of the "Y" hand rests on the temple and then rotates forward. You can use one or both hands.

Crab

The index fingers open and close on the thumbs repeatedly, like claws pinching.

Cracker

The fist of the base hand is held
against the opposite shoulder,
as the action hand forms a fist
and strikes the elbow of the
base hand several times.

Crayon

 Combine the signs **COLOR + WRITE:**

COLOR: Wriggle upturned fingers in front of mouth.

WRITE: The right hand pretends to write on the left palm.

Cry

The index fingers alternately move down the cheeks, like tears rolling down.

Cup

The pinkie side of the "C" hand taps
the opposite palm several times.

Daddy

The thumb of the sideways "5" hand taps the middle of the forehead several times. Fingertips may wiggle.

Dance

The first two fingers of the action hand form an inverted "V" and swing rhythmically back and forth over the up-turned palm of the base hand.

Danger

Both fists are held closed in the "A" handshape. One hand thrusts up suddenly and brushes past the other fist, representing something happening suddenly and unexpectedly.

Deer

The thumbs of the open hands tap the temples a couple of times, indicating the antlers of a deer.

Diaper

Both hands are held at the hips as the first two fingers open and close on the thumbs, indicating diaper pins opening and closing.

Dinosaur

The action hand is held upright with the fingers resting on the thumb. The hand slowly turns from side to side like a dinosaur's head.

Dirty

Hold hand under chin and wiggle fingers. (You're in dirt up to your neck!)

Dog

The hand pats the knee and/or
snaps the fingers, as if calling a dog.

Doll

The bent forefinger is
pulled twice down the nose.

Dolphin

The "B" handshape makes repeated
up and down diving movements in
front of the downturned left arm.

Door
(open/close the door)

The "B" hands face outward, edges touching. Then one moves back and then closed again to show the movement of a door. To say "open the door," leave it open; to say "close the door," start in the open position and close it.

Down

Use the natural gesture:
Index finger points down.

Dream

The index finger opens and closes as it moves away from the temple, like fleeting thoughts drifting away.

Dress

 The fingertips of the open hands brush down
the torso twice, showing the drape of the fabric.

Drink

The signer tips an
imaginary glass to the
open lips as if drinking.

Drum

The hands go through the
motion of playing a drum
with drumsticks.

Dry

 The index finger drags across
the chin as if drying it.

Duck

The action hand is held
near the mouth, facing
out, while the first two
fingers open and close
on top of the thumb,
indicating a duck's bill.

Eat

The fingers and thumb, held together as if holding a small piece of food, tap the mouth several times.

Elephant

Starting at the nose, the "C" hand traces the shape of an elephant's trunk.

Excited

The middle fingers move up the chest, alternately and repeatedly. This is similar to the sign for the word *feel*, which uses just one hand. **EXCITED** means "lots of feeling!"

Fall Down

The first two fingers make an upside-down "V" on the opposite hand, representing a person standing. They then "fall" off the hand.

Family

The forefingers and thumbs of the two "F" hands touch, then separate and come forward in a circular movement until the little fingers touch. I like to think of this as a "circle of love."

Fan

The index finger is held up, turning round and round, representing the motion of a fan.

232

Fast

The thumb-tips flick quickly off of the tips
of the index fingers—sort of like snapping
fingers using your index fingers and thumbs.

Finished ("all done")

Both "5" hands are held palms up,
and then flip over in one swift motion.

Fire

The palms of the open hands face the body and move up and down with fingers wiggling to represent flickering flames.

Firefighter

The "B" handshape is placed on the forehead, representing the shape of a firefighter's hat.

Fire Truck

Sign **FIRE + CAR.**

Fish

Hold your hand on its side and make it "swim" away from you, like a fish moving through the water.

Flower

The fingers and thumb
of the action hand are
held together as if holding
a tiny flower by the stem.
The hand moves from one
side of the nose to the other
as if smelling the flower.

Fly (Bird)

The hands flap like a bird's wings.

Fly (Insect)

Make an "F" handshape by bringing your thumb and forefinger together. Then make it wiggle around in the air in front of you like a fly buzzing around.

Friend

The index fingers lock together; then change positions and lock the opposite way.

Frog

The back of the fist is held under
the chin as the first two fingers
flick outward repeatedly, showing
how the skin of a frog's throat expands.

243

Fruit

Pinch your index finger and thumb together at the corner of your mouth in the "F" handshape. Then twist as if you're twisting the stem off a cherry that's in your mouth.

Frustrated

The back of the flat hand comes up in front of the face, as the head moves backward slightly, like having a door slammed in your face.

no!

Fun

Hold the first two fingers of the action hand together in the "U" handshape. Brush them against the tip of your nose and then bring them down on the first two fingers of the base hand, which are also held in the "U" handshape.

Funny

The first two fingers are held in the "U" handshape and brush against the end of your nose, like you're tickling someone's nose with a feather to make them laugh.

Game

 The two fists, with the thumbs
pointing up, strike each other twice.

Gentle

One hand strokes the back of the opposite hand. (This is similar to **PET.**)

Get

The loosely open hands come together suddenly in two fists, one above the other, as if grabbing something.

Ghost

The index fingers and thumbs come together to make two "F" hands, one above the other with fingers touching. The upper hand then rises in a circular motion, as if pulling a string. This suggests a spirit rising up.

Giraffe

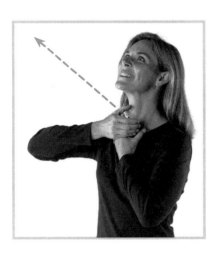 

 The "C" hand starts at the neck and moves up, tracing the shape of giraffe's neck.

Girl

The thumb strokes along the jaw from below the ear to the chin, showing where the ribbon of a bonnet would lie.

Give

The thumb and fingers are held together as if holding something, and the hand moves away from the signer as if giving some-thing away. You can use one or both hands.

Give Me

The thumb and fingers are held together as if holding something. The hand starts a distance away from the body and then moves in closer, as if taking something from someone.

Glasses

The thumbs and index fingers
indicate the outline of glasses.

Go

 Both hands, with index fingers extended, bend at the wrists and point in the direction one is going.

Goat

 Make a "V" with the first two fingers slightly bent, and quickly touch the chin and then the forehead. This represents a goat's beard and horns.

258

Good

 The fingertips of the flat hand touch the lips or chin and then drop forward, landing palm up on the opposite palm. This suggests something that tastes good being offered to another.

Goose

The four fingers of the action hand open and close on the thumb, representing the bill of a goose. This is similar to **DUCK.**

Grandma

The "5" hand is held sideways with the thumb touching the chin. The hand then moves downward and away in two arcs (similar to **MOMMY,** but with two arcs, which symbolize two generations).

Grandpa

The "5" hand is held sideways with the thumb touching the forehead. The hand then moves downward and away in two arcs (similar to **DADDY,** but with two arcs, which symbolize two generations).

Grapes

The slightly bent, open fingers of the action hand bounce down the back of the opposite hand several times, representing the bumpy shape of a cluster of grapes.

Grass

The hand moves palm up
under the chin and brushes
the underside of the chin
twice. It represents an
animal eating hay or grass.

Green

Make a "G" handshape by holding your hand sideways with your thumb and forefinger almost touching, as if you're about to pinch something. Shake the "G" hand to the right, in the space off the right shoulder. (This is the area where some color signs are made.)

Guinea Pig

 The index finger of the action "G" hand brushes the tip of the nose twice, and then the sign for **PIG** is made by flapping the hand up and down underneath the chin in a waving motion.

Guitar

This is easy—just pretend to play an imaginary guitar!

Halloween

Make "V" hands with both hands near the eyes; then pull them outward and closed, symbolizing a Halloween mask.

Hammer

The action hand goes through the motion of swinging a hammer two times.

Hamster

The index finger of the
action "H" hand brushes
the tip of the nose twice.

Hanukkah

The thumb sides of the outward-facing "B" hands come together and then move apart as the fingers spread open, representing candles in a menorah.

Happy

The flat hand pats the chest repeatedly with an upward-stroking movement, representing happy feelings bubbling up.

Hat

Pat your head, showing
where your hat goes.

Hear

Use the natural gesture:
The index finger points to
the ear. You may observe
your baby doing this naturally in response to sounds,
even before you do it.

Helicopter

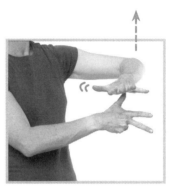

There are two versions of helicopter.
1. The "5" hand is held palm down and quivers as it's pushed up by the tip of the opposite index finger.
2. The "5" hand is held palm down and quivers as it's pushed up by the thumb of the opposite "3" hand.

Hello

The action "B" hand moves outward from the temple in a little salute.

Help

ASL version

Non-ASL version

ASL version
The action hand, formed into a fist, is placed on top of the flat base hand. Both rise up together as if the flat hand is helping to lift the fist. The thumb may point upward and can be used to indicate who needs help by pointing as it rises.

Non-ASL version
This alternate version is recommended for very young children by Joseph Garcia in his book *Sign with your Baby.* Both flat hands pat the chest. This is a great frustration reducer for even the littlest signers.

Hide

The "A" fist ducks under
the opposite palm to "hide."

Hill

The flat, downturned action hand outlines the shape of a hill.

Hippopotamus

Extend the index and little fingers of each hand to form two "Y" handshapes. Make the hands open and close on each other like a big mouth opening. The extended fingers are the hippo's big teeth.

Home

The fingers and thumb, brought together to form a flattened "O," move from the side of the mouth to the cheek. This is a variation of **EAT** and **SLEEP.**

Hooray!
(also *Yippee! Yahoo! Excellent!*)

Raise both open hands up in the air and shake them as you cheer "Hooray!" This is the ASL version of clapping. If you think about it, the whole point of clapping is to make a loud noise—there's no point to clapping if you're deaf! Hence, the raised-hands-shaking sign for *hooray!*

Horse

The thumb touches the temple while the extended first two fingers flap up and down together, like a horse's ear. You can use one or both hands.

Hot

The signer holds the hand like a claw, palm facing the mouth, and then drops the palm downward as if spitting out hot food and throwing it on the floor.

House

 The flat hands trace an outline
of a house with a pointed roof.

Hug

Cross your arms over your
chest and hug them in close as
you hunch your shoulders and
twist from side to side a little.
You can also wrap your hands
farther around your body to
show a bigger hug.

Hungry

The bent fingers of the action hand move from the throat straight down to the chest, representing the path that food travels.

Ice Cream

The hand moves in front of the mouth as if licking an ice-cream cone. When doing this with babies and children, I stick my tongue out and pretend to lick.

I Love You

This can be signed as three separate signs or by using a single gesture.

I: Index finger points to self.

LOVE: Fists cross over the chest at wrists.

YOU: Index finger points to the other person.

I LOVE YOU: Hold up the "Y" hand, with the index finger extended.

In

One hand pretends
to put something
in the other.

Juice

 Sign **DRINK** by tipping the action "C" hand to the mouth, and then draw an imaginary "J" in the air with your little finger.

Jump

The first two fingers
of the action hand
form an inverted "V"
on the palm of the base hand.
The action hand springs
up and down, representing
legs jumping.

Keys

The index finger
of the action hand bends
at the knuckle and turns
in the sideways palm
of the base hand,
representing
a key turning in a lock.

Kiss

The hand touches the mouth and then the cheek,
as if putting a kiss on the cheek.

Know

The fingertips of the
downturned action hand
touch the temple, indicating
that there's knowledge
in the brain.

Laugh

The index fingers of the
"L" handshapes start at the
corners of the mouth
and brush back off the
face several times
as the signer
smiles.

oh ha ho hee ha!

Light (On/Off/Flashing)

The raised hand bends down at the wrist with tips of fingers and thumb held together. The fingers then open, representing rays of light shining down.

Variations: Open fingers mean **LIGHT ON,** and closed fingers mean **LIGHT OFF.** Both hands opening and closing, repeatedly and quickly, mean **FLASHING LIGHTS.**

Like

 The thumb and middle finger of the action hand come together in a pinching motion close to the chest, and then the hand moves outward.

Lion

Bend your fingers to make a "claw hand" and sweep your hand from the front of your head to the back, outlining the mane of a lion.

Little

The sideways-held hands move toward and away from each other, indicating that something is small.

Lizard

The index finger of the
right "L" hand "squiggles"
up the opposite arm.

Look

 The first two fingers form a "V," pointing at the eyes and then moving away toward what you're looking at.

Loud

Combine the signs **HEAR** and **SHAKE** to mean that the sound was so loud it shook the ground!

Me

Point to yourself.

Meat

The thumb and forefinger
of the action hand pinch
the "meaty" part of the
opposite hand, between
the thumb and forefinger.

Milk

 The sideways-held fist is opened
and closed several times, as if
milking a cow.

Mine/My

The palm of the action hand moves toward the chest, coming to rest there.

Mirror

The action "B" hand
is held in front of the face,
twisting from side to
side several times,
as if looking at
yourself in a mirror.

Mommy

The thumb of the
sideways "5" hand
taps the chin several times.
Fingertips may wiggle.

Monkey

The hands scratch up
and down on
the sides, imitating
a monkey.

Moon

The signer gazes up at his raised hand, which forms a crescent with only the thumb and forefinger.

More

The thumbs and fingertips of each hand are held together, and the fingertips of both hands tap together several times. This represents gathering more things together.

Morning

The left arm (base arm) is held palm up across the torso with the hand resting in the crook of the upturned right arm (action arm). The right forearm rises slowly, representing the sun coming up over the horizon.

Mountain

 Sign the word rock by placing one
downturned fist on top of the other.
Then open the hands and move them
up to the left at an angle, representing
the side of a mountain.

Mouse

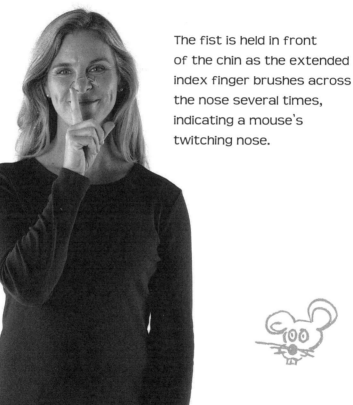

The fist is held in front of the chin as the extended index finger brushes across the nose several times, indicating a mouse's twitching nose.

Movie

The action "5" hand slides quickly from side to side across the opposite palm, representing the frames of a film moving through the projector.

Music/Sing

The action hand, held on its side, moves rhythmically back and forth over the forearm, which is held in front of the chest.

Naughty

 The fingertips of the flat action hand touch the lips and then turn away and drop downward as if tasting something bad and then turning it away. Be sure to make a face that says, "This behavior doesn't agree with me!"

Nice (same as Clean)

The downturned hand wipes dirt off of the opposite upturned hand in one smooth motion.
(This is also used for **CLEAN.**)

Night

The left arm is held across the body, palm down. With one wrist on top of the other, the downturned right "B" hand slowly moves downward, as if to show the sun going down over the horizon.

No

no!
no! NO

The first two fingers
close down on the thumb.
This is a variation of
the finger spelling
of N-O.

No Touch

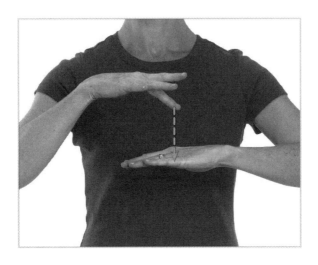

Sign **NO** and then **TOUCH:**
The middle finger drops down
to touch the back of
the opposite hand.

Ocean

Combine the signs for **WATER** and waves.
Tap the action "W" hand once on the chin.
Then make a wavelike motion, moving out
from your body, with the downward-facing palms.

Off

One flat hand moves
off of the other.
(**Note:** This is *not* the sign
for turn off.)

On

One flat hand moves
onto the other.
(**Note:** This is *not* the sign
for turn on.)

Open

The outward-facing "B" hands start in the closed position, then open and drop down slightly.

Orange
(Color or Fruit)

 Pretend to squeeze the juice
from an orange into your mouth.

Out/Outside

 For out, one hand moves out of the other.
To indicate outside, repeat the motion.

Owl

Put both "O" hands over your eyes like binoculars and rotate them in and then out twice. This represents an owl's big eyes.

Pacifier

Make a modified "c"
hand with just the thumb
and forefinger of the
action hand. Move it
toward your mouth
several times as if
putting a pacifier
into the mouth.

Pain

 1. PAIN: The two index fingers tap together several times at the location of the pain, representing throbbing nerve endings. The face should show a pained expression.

2. EARACHE: This is an example of localizing the sign at the sight of the path.

Pants

Go through the motion of pulling up pants.

Party

Swing both "P" handshapes
from side to side.

Penguin

Move the shoulders alternately up and down with the hands sticking out on either side of the waist, showing the movement a penguin makes while walking.

Pet

One hand strokes the back
of the opposite hand.
(This is similar to **GENTLE**.)

Piano

Go through the motions of playing a piano.

Pie

 The sideways-held action hand makes two diagonal slicing motions on the opposite flat palm, as if cutting a pie.

Pig

The hand flaps up and down underneath the chin in a waving motion, representing food dripping from the mouth of a pig. This is similar to **DIRTY,** which has wiggling fingers.

Pink

The "P" handshape points to the lips and then moves downward. This is similar to **RED.**

Play

The "Y" hands are shaken, pivoting at the wrists, representing the shaking of a tambourine.

Please

The open palm touches
the chest and moves
in a circular motion.

Police Officer

The right "C" handshape taps the left side of the chest, where a police officer's badge would go. The "C" stands for "caring"—or if it helps you remember, think of "cop."

Poop

 Pull the thumb out of the bottom of the opposite closed fist.

Potato

The first two fingers of the
"V" hand bend at the knuckles
and then tap the back of
the opposite closed fist,
representing sticking a fork
into a potato.

Pray

The hands are held in
a gesture of prayer.

Present/Gift

 Start by making two upright "X" handshapes by bending your forefingers; then swing them down and forward in an arc, as if handing a gift to someone.

Princess

The "P" handshape outlines the sash worn by a princess.

Proud

The thumb of the
"A" hand moves
up the chest, indicating
the feeling of pride welling
up inside.

348

Pumpkin

The middle finger of the
action hand flicks the back
of the opposite fist as
if tapping a pumpkin to
see if it's ripe.

Purple

Make a "P" handshape by drooping the index finger downward at an angle, and then shake your "P" hand in the area off your right shoulder.
(This is the area where some color signs are made.)

Purse

The signer mimes holding a purse by the handle and bouncing it up and down a couple of times.

Quiet

Start by making the "Shhh" sign with one index finger in front of the other near your lips.
Then open the hands and push them down flat, as if pushing down the noise.

Rabbit/Bunny

Raise the first two fingers, holding them together in the "U" handshape. Hold them at your temples and make them twitch back a couple of times. You can use one or both hands.

Raccoon

 Make two "V" handshapes near your eyes, like the mask of a raccoon, and then move then outward to the sides of the face, changing them to "R" handshapes.

Rain

 The hands are held palms down with fingers spread and bent. They make a double downward movement, representing rain falling.

Rainbow

 The left "4" handshape is held upright.
The fingertips of the right "4" handshape
touch the fingertips of the left and then move
up and across an arc, representing a rainbow.

Rat

The crossed first two fingers of the "R" handshape brush the tip of the nose twice.

Rattle

The hand mimics
shaking a rattle.

Read

The first two fingers form a "V,"
representing the eyes,
which scan the flat palm
of the opposite hand,
as if reading it.

Red

The index finger points to the lips and then moves downward, indicating the red color of the lips.

Rock

One "A" hand taps the back
of the opposite flat hand.

Roll

The index fingers
roll over one another
as they move forward.

Run

Start with two "L" hands, the right slightly behind the left. Hook the index finger of the right "L" hand around the thumb of the left "L" hand. Both hands move forward quickly, with the forefingers and thumbs wiggling.

Sad

The open hands are held palm in, in front of the face; then move them down as the head droops slightly, and make a sad face.

Santa Claus

 Start with two bent "5" hands at your cheeks
and then move them down in an arc,
representing Santa's big, full beard.

Scared

 The fists face each other and then suddenly move together with palms opening and fingers shaking. A startled expression on the face is important.

School

Clap the hands twice, with the right hand on top of the left, representing a teacher who's trying to get the students' attention.

Search

The action "C" hand moves in circles in front of the face as the face moves to the side. Imagine a lookout in the crow's nest of a ship searching the horizon with a spyglass.

See

 The first two fingers form a "V," representing the eyes. They move forward, showing the concept of seeing. (Also see **LOOK.**)

Shake

The two fists move back and forth as if shaking something.

Shampoo

The fingers go through the motion of massaging shampoo into the scalp.

Share

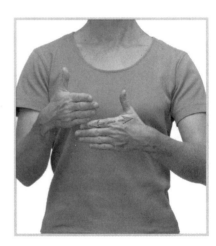

The little finger of the side-facing action hand brushes back and forth along the index finger of the sideways base hand, which has its thumb extended. This represents dividing things up to be shared.

Shave

The bent forefinger of the "X" handshape moves down the side of the face, pretending to shave it.

Sheep

Make your first two fingers
into an imaginary pair of
scissors and clip "wool" off
of your left downturned arm.

Shirt

Indicate the shirt by
pulling on the front of it.
You can use one or
both hands.

Shoes

The thumb sides of
the fists tap together,
representing someone
clicking the heels of their
shoes together.

Shout

 The bent fingers of the "5" handshape start at the mouth and then move outward, representing the loud noise coming out.

Sick

The middle fingers of
the "5" hands bend inward
and touch the forehead
and stomach at the
same time. Make a face that
says, "I feel sick!"

Sign

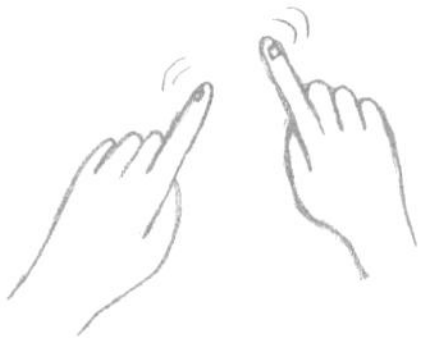

The index fingers
are extended upward
and move in alternating
circles, representing
the motion of the hands
when a person is signing.

Silly

Raise the thumb and little finger
to make a "Y" handshape.
Twist it in front of your face,
brushing the thumb
against your nose.

Sister

The action "L" hand starts at the chin and then moves down to rest on top of the opposite "L" hand. Some people make the sign for **GIRL** before doing this part.

Sit

The first two fingers of the action hand form a "V" and then bend at the knuckles to "sit" on the first two fingers of the base hand.

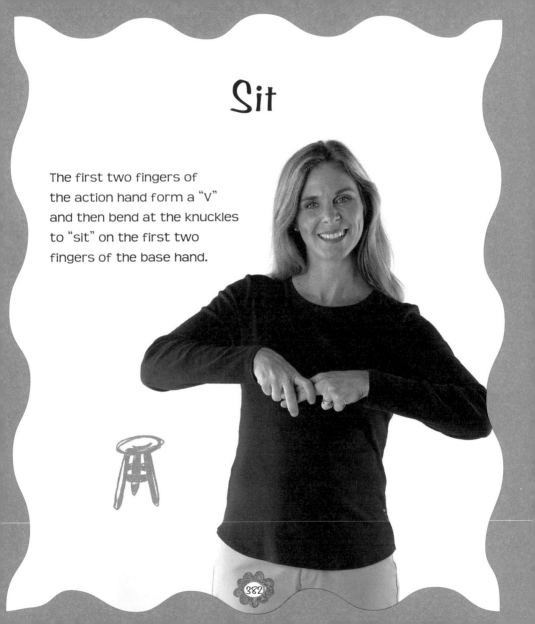

Skunk

The "K" handshape moves from forehead to the back of the head, indicating the white stripe of a skunk.

Sleep

 The "5" hand is held in front of the face. It then moves down as the fingers close and the head droops, representing someone closing her eyes and falling asleep.

Slide

The first two fingers of the action are held in a "V" shape, representing legs. They "slide" down the first two fingers of the opposite hand, which are held together and represent a playground slide.

Slow

One flat hand moves slowly
up the back of the other,
from fingertips to wrist.

Smell

Move your palm up toward your nose using a double, slightly circular movement. Imagine wafting the aroma from a pot of soup toward your nose.

Snake

The first two fingers are bent to look like the fangs of a snake. The hand moves down and away from the mouth as it curves back and forth like a snake slithering.

Snow

The hands move down as they sway
side to side with fingers fluttering.

Soap

The fingertips move in a circle in the palm of the opposite hand, as if lathering soap.

Socks

The index fingers point downward and alternately slide against each other, similar to knitting needles making socks.

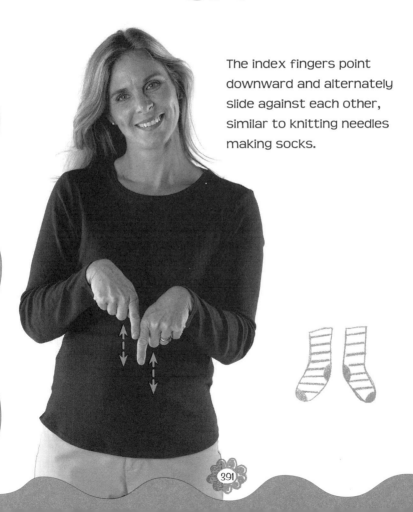

Soft

With the palms up, bring the
fingers together gently as if
showing that something
has a soft consistency.

Sorry

The fist moves in
a circular motion
on the chest.

Spaghetti/Noodles

The pinkie fingers make little circles as they move apart.

Spider

Pinkie fingers are locked together and the rest of the fingers wiggle as your hands move forward.

Splash

 The fists are brought together in front of the body and then move up and outward, as the fingers splay open with palms facing out to represent a big splash.

Squirrel

Make two bent "V" handshapes by bending the first two fingers at the knuckles. Tap them together several times near the mouth to represent a squirrel gnawing on a nut.

Starfish

Sign **STARS** + **FISH.**

Stars

The two index fingers rub against each other as they point alternately skyward. This represents stars twinkling.

Stick

Bring your thumbs and forefingers together to make two "F" handshapes, and then slide them apart, showing the shape and length of a stick.

Sticker

Go through the motion of peeling a sticker off the palm of your hand.

Sticky

The thumbs and forefingers
open and close as if feeling
something sticky.

Stink

Pinch your nose shut
to show that something
is stinky.

Stone

The "A" handshape taps the back of the opposite, downturned, flat hand.

Stop

The edge of one hand comes down on the palm of the other, representing something coming to a quick stop.

Store/Sell

The fingers and thumbs are held together, making the flat "O" handshape. They point to the body and then twist outward at the wrists. This represents holding up something that you're selling. If you do the wrist motion only once it means **SELL.** Repeated multiple times, it means **STORE.** When signing with hearing babies, we tend to repeat motions a lot anyway to ensure that baby sees the sign, but it's good to know this difference for your own information.

Story

Bring the thumbs and index fingers of both hands together repeatedly in a circular motion, slightly linking them each time and then pulling them apart. This represents words being strung together to make a story.

Sun

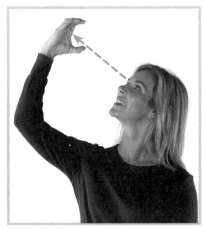

The "c" hand taps the temple and then rises up over the head as you gaze up at it. Notice that for **SUN,** the whole hand forms the crescent shape, whereas for **MOON,** a crescent is made with only the thumb and forefinger.

Swim

 Go through the motions
of the breaststroke.

Swing

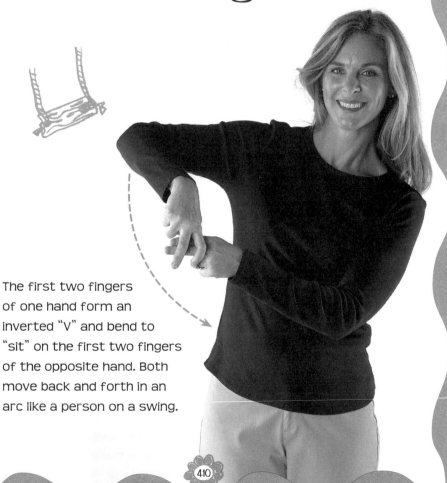

The first two fingers
of one hand form an
inverted "V" and bend to
"sit" on the first two fingers
of the opposite hand. Both
move back and forth in an
arc like a person on a swing.

410

Tea

The action "F" hand stirs an imaginary tea bag around in a cup formed by the opposite "C" hand.

Teacher

Combine the signs for **TEACH** and **PERSON.** Sign **TEACH** by making two flat "O" hands by bringing the fingers and your thumbs together in a circle and then flattening the "O" out. Move these outward from the temples. Then sign **PERSON** by changing them to "B" hands and moving them straight down the sides of the body.

Telephone

The "Y" hand is held to
the side of the head,
representing a telephone.

Thank You
and You're Welcome

The fingertips of the flat hand touch the lips and then move out and down toward the person being thanked, representing nice words coming from the mouth.

Thirsty

The index finger draws an imaginary line down the throat. This represents liquid running down the throat.

Throw

 The hand starts near the face with fingertips and thumb together in a flattened "O" handshape. The hand then opens as it moves forward as if throwing something.

Tickle

Wiggle the fingers of both hands, smiling mischievously, as if you're about to tickle someone.

Tiger

 The bent fingers of both hands are pulled across
the face, representing a tiger's stripes.

Toilet/Potty

Shake the fist with
the thumb tucked between
the first two fingers.
This is the "T" handshape
for *toilet*.

Toothbrush/Brush Teeth

The signer mimes scrubbing
teeth with the index finger.

Towel

Pretend to pull an imaginary towel back and forth behind you, as if drying your back.

421

Toy

Make two fists with your thumbs between your first two fingers. These are "T" hands. Shake your "T" hands.

Tractor

Pretend to grasp a steering wheel (as in **CAR**) while bouncing your entire body as if driving a tractor over bumpy ground.

Train

Both hands are held in the "U" or "V" handshape, and the fingers of one hand move back and forth on the fingers of the other, representing the tracks and railway ties.

Tree

The elbow of the
action hand rests on the
opposite open palm with
fingers splayed open ("5" hand)
to represent the branches
of a tree. The hand pivots
back and forth at the wrist.

Truck

The two fists mimic driving a large steering wheel. It's similar to **CAR,** but with a bigger steering wheel.

Try

Make two "T" handshapes with your thumbs sticking out through the first two fingers of each hand. Push them forward and arc slightly upward at the end as if pushing through something difficult. (*Variation:* This sign is sometimes done with "S" or "A" hands.)

Turtle

The action "A" hand is covered by the opposite downturned hand. The thumb of the "A" hand moves up and down twice, representing a turtle's head. The downturned hand represents the shell.

Uncle

The action "U" hand makes a small, circular movement near the temple.

Up

The index finger
of the action
hand points
straight up.

Vegetable

The action "V" handshape is twisted at the corner of the mouth.

Violin

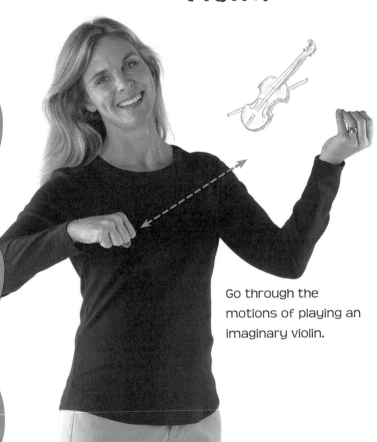

Go through the
motions of playing an
imaginary violin.

Wagon

The upturned action
fist goes through the
motion of pulling a wagon.

Wait

One hand is held slightly in front of the other as the fingers flutter.

Walk

 The downturned palms move alternately toward and away from the chest, representing the movement of walking feet.

Want

 Extend the fingers of both hands forward with your palms up, and then pull back as your fingers close, as if pulling something toward yourself. Many babies do this sign naturally, without being taught.

Warm

The closed fist is held close to the mouth and then opens as it moves away, representing warm breath coming from the mouth.

Wash

The closed fist scrubs the
opposite open palm in a
circular motion, as if
washing something.

Wash Hands

Rub hands all over each other as if washing them.

Water

The index, middle, and ring
finger are extended to form
a "W" hand. The "W" taps
the chin twice.

Wet

The ASL sign for **WET** combines the signs **WATER** and **SOFT,** which is made by opening and closing the fingers. For simplicity's sake, you might sometimes abbreviate it and just do the opening and closing fingers part, as if you're feeling the wetness on your fingertips. I especially like to do this when I'm singing a song to my baby with the **WET** sign.

What

The hands are raised palms up in the natural "What?" gesture.

Where

The hand, index finger
extended, waves from
side to side in a small arc.

White

The open palm is placed against the chest
and then pulled straight out as the
fingertips come together.

Wind

 Both open hands are held sideways in front of the body. The hands sway gracefully from side to side like trees blowing in the wind.

Work

Form both hands into "S" handshapes by making fists with the thumbs lying across the knuckles. With the palms facing down, tap one wrist on the other a few times, as if hammering.

Worm

The action index finger bends and straightens as it moves across the opposite sideways-held palm.

Yellow

Make a "Y" hand
by raising only your
thumb and pinkie. Shake
the "Y" hand in the space
off your right shoulder.
(This is the area where
some color signs are done.)

Yes

The action "S" hand
"nods" up and down,
like a head nodding.

Zebra

 Sign **HORSE** and then indicate stripes by pulling the "4" hand across the body.

acknowledgments

I'd like to thank Drs. Linda Acredolo and Susan Goodwyn for their pioneering research in the field of baby sign language. I'd also like to thank Dr. Joseph Garcia and the entire staff of Sign2Me/ Northlight Communications for all their incredible support and encouragement in getting my classes up and running; and Drs. Michelle Anthony and Reyna Lindert for their wonderfully designed curriculum and for their personal encouragement. Last but not least, I want to thank all the members of the

Sign2Me™ Presenters' Network for sharing ideas, encouragement, and support. Together we're making baby sign language available to everyone who has contact with a preverbal child.

resources

ASL Websites

Here are some awesome resources you just *have* to check out! Whether you're looking for a new sign, you'd like some signing support from other parents and teachers, or you just want an online forum to brag about your baby's first sign, you can find a wealth of free information on the Internet!

American Sign Language Browser, **www.commtechlab .msu.edu/sites/aslweb/browser.htm.** This is one of my favorite Websites for looking up signs. It's also great for clarifying what you see in a printed dictionary because it shows a little video of each sign being demonstrated!

ASL University, **www.lifeprint.com**. This is another excellent resource! You can look up signs from the vast online dictionary or even take a free ASL course.

Sign with Sam, **www.signwithsam.com**. This supercute site features Sam, an animated signing toddler. There are games, printable pages for coloring, and a store, too.

SIGN *with your* BABY Yahoo! Group, **http://groups.yahoo.com/group/Sign withyourbaby/**. This is the best and biggest online forum for parents and teachers who are interested in using ASL with babies and young children. Use this site to find answers to your signing questions or just to brag about your baby's brilliant signing achievements!

Baby Sign Language Books and Kits

Sign, Sing, and Play! Fun Signing Activities for You and Your Baby, by Monta Z. Briant (Hay House, Inc., Carlsbad, CA, 2006). This book picks up where *Baby Sign Language Basics* leaves off. The secret to signing success is Make signing fun!" This book is packed with imaginative ideas for including signing in every aspect of Baby's life, whether it's bath time, a trip to the playground, or shopping at the grocery store. Includes clear photos of 165 ASL signs!

The Sign, Sing, and Play Kit, by Monta Z. Briant (Hay House, Inc., Carlsbad, CA, 2006). This kit includes everything you need to have the most fun ever signing with your baby! Includes the book *Sign, Sing, and Play!;* the *Songs for Little Hands* music CD, featuring original signing songs by award-winning singer/songwriter Susan Z; the illustrated *Songs for Little Hands Activity Guide* with signs and lyrics to accompany the CD; and a set of 50 ASL flash cards—all packed in a sturdy box!

Sign with your Baby, by Joseph Garcia (Northlight Communications, Seattle, WA, 1999). Originally published under the title *Toddler Talk* in 1994, this was *the first* baby sign language book. I guess you could call Joseph Garcia the "Father of Baby Sign Language," but this very modest fellow would probably blush and get all teary eyed, and tell you not to make such a big deal about it. Well, it *is* a big deal, and he's a great guy—and it's *still* a great book! Also look for the *Sign with your Baby: Complete Learning Kit,* which includes the book, an instructional video, and a laminated reference chart. It's available at bookstores, **Amazon.com,** or **www.sign2me.com**.

Signing Smart with Babies and Toddlers, by Michelle E. Anthony, M.A., Ph.D., and Reyna Lindert, Ph.D. (St. Martin's Press, New York, NY, 2005). Anthony and Lindert's Signing Smart method is a simple, straightforward, and intelligent ASL technique for signing with babies; and it's compatible with other ASL methods. The book contains many fun signing activities and songs.

Dancing with Words: Signing for Hearing Children's Literacy, by Marilyn Daniels (Bergin & Garvey, Westport, CT, 2001). This *excellent* book focuses on how signing with children enhances literacy and reading skills.

Baby Signs: How to Talk to Your Baby Before Your Baby Can Talk, by Linda Acredolo, Ph.D., and Susan Goodwyn, Ph.D., with Douglas Abrams (McGraw-Hill/Contemporary Books, New York, NY, 2002). Drs. Acredolo and Goodwyn conducted a long-term study on using signing with hearing babies that was funded by the National Institutes of Health. This book contains their findings and also includes developmental information, strategies, and signing activities. There's only one drawback: Many of the signs included aren't actual ASL signs.

ASL Dictionaries

American Sign Language Dictionary, by Martin L. A. Sternberg (HarperCollins, New York, NY, 1998). Available in full or concise versions.

Random House Webster's American Sign Language Dictionary, by Elaine Costello, Ph.D. (Random House, New York, NY, 1999). Available in full, concise, and pocket versions. The pocket version is the best because of its tiny size and *plastic cover!* Don't leave home without it!

Sign Language for Kids: A Fun & Easy Guide to American Sign Language, by Laura Heller (Sterling, New York, NY, 2004). This is an excellent hardcover book with full-color photos of ASL signs.

Signs for Me: Basic Sign Vocabulary for Children, Parents & Teachers, by Ben Bahan and Joe Dannis (DawnSignPress, San Diego, CA, 1990). This book of kid-friendly signs is organized grammatically and thematically. The signers in the pictures are children, and the large illustrations are suitable for coloring.

Teach Your Tot to Sign, by Stacy A. Thompson, illustrated by Valerie Nelson-Metlay (Gallaudet University Press, Washington, D.C., 2005). This wonderful little book is actually a complete *baby sign language dictionary* with more than 500 signs appropriate for babies and kids of all ages!

Children's Books

Amazon.com has the widest selection.

An Alphabet of Animal Signs, by S. Harold Collins et al. (Garlic Press, Eugene, OR, 2001). Contains an animal sign for each letter of the alphabet.

Animal Signs: A First Book of Sign Language, by Debby Slier (Gallaudet University Press, Washington, D.C., 1995). This board book contains illustrations and corresponding signs.

Baby's First Signs, More Baby's First Signs, A Book of Colors, and *Out for a Walk,* by Kim Votry and Kurt Waller (Gallaudet University Press, Washington, D.C., 2001–2003). These are four beautiful board books! Get the whole series! *My First Book of Sign Language,* by Joan Holub (Troll Communications, Memphis, TN, 1998).

My First Book of Sign Language, by Joan Holub (Troll Communications, Memphis, TN, 1998).

Opposites: A Beginner's Book of Signs and *Happy Birthday: A Beginner's Book of Signs,* by Angela Bednarczyk and Janet Weinstock (Star Bright Books, Long Island City, NY, 1997). These board books contain object photos and corresponding signs.

Pets, Animals & Creatures, by S. Harold Collins et al. (Garlic Press, Eugene, OR, 2001). Contains photographs and signs for 77 pets, farm animals, and wild animals. Garlic Press has many other wonderful signing books for children, too! Check out **www.garlicpress.com**.

Simple Signs, by Cindy Wheeler (Puffin Books, London, England, 1997).

Word Signs: A First Book of Sign Language, by Debby Slier (Gallaudet University Press, Washington, D.C., 1995). This board book contains object photos and corresponding signs.

You Can Learn Sign Language! by Jackie Kramer and Tali Ovadia (Troll Communications, Memphis, TN, 2000).

Videos/DVDs

Baby Sign Language Basics: Early Communication for Hearing Babies and Toddlers Instructional DVD (Hay House, 2009).

Baby Einstein: My First Signs (Walt Disney Video, 2007). Additional titles in this series include *Around the House* and *Baby's Favorite Places.*

Baby See 'n Sign: Volume 1 (Kronz Kidz Productions, 2004). This is an excellent learning video with more than 60 signs for babies and toddlers.

Baby See 'n Sign: Volume 2 (Kronz Kidz Productions, 2004). The second volume is also a terrific learning video with more than *100* signs for babies and toddlers, including a bonus signing section on manners!

Blue's Clues: All Kinds of Signs (Paramount Studios, 2001).

Happy Signs Day: Sign Language for Babies and Toddlers (Language Tree, 2006). *Happy Signs Night* is also available.

Sign-A-Lot: The Big Surprise and *Sign-A-Lot: ABC Games* (Barbara Granoff and Lee Sher, **www.signalot.com**). These are great DVDs showing mostly elementary-age kids signing. Both my toddler and my seven-year-old enjoy watching these!

Signing Time! Volumes 1–13 and *Baby Signing Time!* Volumes 1–2 (Two Little Hands Productions, 2002–2006, **www.signingtime.com**). This is an amazing collection, featuring a deaf preschooler and her hearing toddler cousin. I have to say that these are the very best children's entertainment videos/DVDs that I've ever seen—signing or not! Their quality is wonderful, and they contain beautiful original music and lots and lots of kids of all ages and abilities using signs. Many PBS (public television) stations nationwide have picked up this series—check your local listings or **www.signingtime.com** to see if it's being broadcast in your area!

Talking Hands: A Sign Language Video for Children (Small Fry Productions, 2000).

Music

"*Songs for Little Hands*" *Activity Guide and CD* (Mylaboo Music, 2004; distributed by Hay House, Inc.). Finally, the perfect music CD for signing with your baby! The 14 songs (11 original, 3 traditional) by award-winning singer/songwriter Susan Z are the perfect length and tempo for signing babies; and the musical style is fun, fresh, and absolutely charming. The accompanying activity guide shows the signs and lyrics for each song for easy learning.

Pick Me Up! Fun Songs for Learning Signs (Northlight Communications, 2003). Music CD and hardcover activity guide with tear-resistant pages. This contains wonderful children's music that won't grate on your nerves, in musical styles reminiscent of Sinatra, The Beach Boys, Elvis, and more. It's available at **www.sign2me.com**.

Other Media

Baby Sign Language Basics Flash Cards, by Monta Z. Briant (Hay House, Inc., 2007) A deck of 50 *beautiful* American Sign Language (ASL) flash cards. The brightly colored photos of real children and objects on the front of the card catch and hold Baby's attention much better than the pastel illustrations on some other card decks. Easy-to-understand color photos on the back show how the sign is done. Babies seem to love looking at both sides equally!

Sign2Me® Reminder Series: Posters/Place mats (Northlight Communications, 2002). The Reminder Series comprises laminated posters in eight themes. Each poster presents concepts in ASL, English, and Spanish and are the perfect size for place mats or posting on walls. They're available at **www.sign2me.com**.

endnotes

Chapter 3

1. *Baby Signs,* Linda Acredolo, Ph.D., and Susan Goodwyn, Ph.D.
2. Ibid.
3. *Dancing with Words: Signing for Hearing Children's Literacy,* Marilyn Daniels.

Chapter 4

1. *Baby Signs,* Linda Acredolo, Ph.D., and Susan Goodwyn, Ph.D.
2. *Save Your Baby: Throw Out Your Equipment,* Laura Sobell.

Chapter 9

1. *Sign with your Baby,* Joseph Garcia.
2. Ibid.
3. Ibid.
4. "Making Every Sign Count," Patricia Spencer, Ph.D., *Perspectives in Educa tion and Deafness,* Vol. 17, No.2.

Chapter 16

1. Sign2Me: **www.sign2me.com** or 877-744-6263.

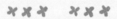

about the author

Monta Z. Briant, a native of San Francisco, California, and her husband, Paul, of Cape Town, South Africa, began signing with their daughter, Sirena, when she was six months old. The family eventually learned hundreds of signs together. Monta was so moved by the experience of being able to communicate effectively with her then-preverbal daughter that she found herself telling anyone pushing a stroller about baby sign language.

In 2001, Monta, a former professional yacht chef and Coast Guard licensed captain, decided to make a permanent career change that would enable her to stay home with her daughter, and she founded Baby Sign Language Workshops. An enthusiastic speaker and self-proclaimed "Baby Sign Language evangelist," Monta teaches workshops and parent-tot signing classes throughout San Diego County and is also available for speaking engagements. Her classes have been the subject of feature stories in the *San Diego Union-Tribune* and on Fox 6 News, KUSI News, and KPBS's *Full Focus.*

In 2004, the Briants welcomed baby Aiden to the family and began signing with him immediately. Big sister Sirena has been a big help with her brother in all ways, and she has especially enjoyed teaching him new signs.

Monta is a member of the Sign2Me™ Presenters' Network and can be reached at **Monta@babysignlanguage.net**. For class schedules and other information, please visit: **www.babysignlanguage.net**.

notes

notes

notes

notes

notes

notes

notes

notes

notes

Hay House Titles of Related Interest

YOU CAN HEAL YOUR LIFE, the movie, starring Louise L. Hay & Friends
(available as a 1-DVD program and an expanded 2-DVD set)
Watch the trailer at: **www.LouiseHayMovie.com**

THE SHIFT, the movie, starring Dr. Wayne W. Dyer
(available as a 1-DVD program and an expanded 2-DVD set)
Watch the trailer at: **www.DyerMovie.com**

✷ ✷ ✷

THE CARE AND FEEDING OF INDIGO CHILDREN, by Doreen Virtue

*THE CRYSTAL CHILDREN: A Guide to the Newest Generation of Psychic
and Sensitive Children,* by Doreen Virtue

INCREDIBLE YOU! 10 Ways to Let Your Greatness Shine Through,
by Dr. Wayne W. Dyer, with Kristina Tracy

IT'S <u>NOT</u> WHAT YOU'VE GOT! Lessons for Kids on Money and Abundance,
by Dr. Wayne W. Dyer, with Kristina Tracy

*THE MOMMY CHRONICLES: Conversations Sharing the Comedy and Drama of Pregnancy and
New Motherhood,* by Sara Ellington and Stephanie Triplett

THANK YOU, ANGELS! by Doreen Virtue, with Kristina Tracy

UNSTOPPABLE ME! 10 Ways to Soar Through Life, by Dr. Wayne W. Dyer,
with Kristina Tracy

*WHAT THEY KNOW ABOUT . . . PARENTING! Celebrity Moms and Dads Give Us Their Take on
Having Kids,* interviews by Cindy Pearlman, edited by Jill Kramer

All of the above are available at your local bookstore,
or may be ordered by contacting Hay House (see last page).

✷ ✷ ✷

We hope you enjoyed this Hay House book. If you'd like to receive our online catalog featuring additional information on Hay House books and products, or if you'd like to find out more about the Hay Foundation, please contact:

Hay House, Inc.
P.O. Box 5100
Carlsbad, CA 92018-5100

(760) 431-7695 or **(800) 654-5126**
(760) 431-6948 (fax) or **(800) 650-5115 (fax)**
www.hayhouse.com® • **www.hayfoundation.org**

Published and distributed in Australia by:
Hay House Australia Pty. Ltd., 18/36 Ralph St., Alexandria NSW 2015
Phone: 612-9669-4299 • Fax: 612-9669-4144 • www.hayhouse.com.au

Published and distributed in the United Kingdom by:
Hay House UK, Ltd., Astley House, 33 Notting Hill Gate,
London W11 3JQ • Phone: 44-20-3675-2450
Fax: 44-20-3675-2451 • www.hayhouse.co.uk

Published and distributed in the Republic of South Africa by:
Hay House SA (Pty), Ltd., P.O. Box 990, Witkoppen 2068
Phone/Fax: 27-11-467-8904 • www.hayhouse.co.za

Published in India by: Hay House Publishers India,
Muskaan Complex, Plot No. 3, B-2, Vasant Kunj, New Delhi 110 070
Phone: 91-11-4176-1620 • Fax: 91-11-4176-1630 • www.hayhouse.co.in

Distributed in Canada by: Raincoast,
9050 Shaughnessy St., Vancouver, B.C. V6P 6E5 • Phone: (604) 323-7100
Fax: (604) 323-2600 • www.raincoast.com

Take Your Soul on a Vacation

Visit **www.HealYourLife.com**® to regroup, recharge, and reconnect with your own magnificence. Featuring blogs, mind-body-spirit news, and life-changing wisdom from Louise Hay and friends.

Visit **www.HealYourLife.com** today!